The

TO H(

The author was born near H
a family with strong links to the Anglican Church. In early childhood he
attended a popular charismatic church, but later moved with his family
to a more traditional church in a neighbouring parish. Following a period
of atheism and agnosticism in his teens, he became Muslim in 1998. He
has a degree in Development from the University of London and a
master's degree from the University of Stirling, and currently works for
the National Health Service. Today he lives in a little house on the side
of a steep valley in the Chiltern Hills with his Hemşin wife.

TO HONOUR GOD

Timothy Bowes

The Othello Press Ltd.

Published by The Othello Press Ltd.
www.othello-press.com

ISBN 978-0-9554818-1-9

Printed and bound in the UK by
Lightning Source, Milton Keynes

In the name of God, the Beneficent, the Merciful

O mankind, indeed We have created you from a male and a female, and made you into nations and tribes that you may know one another. Indeed, the most noble of you in the sight of God is the most righteous of you. And God has knowledge of all things.

Qur'an 49:13

CONTENTS

A Sea Of Reflections

It looked as if there would be no escaping the rain last summer. Some of us managed a week or two away, but got more of the same from a room with a different view—mine was on the beautiful south coast of Ireland. I had received fewer manuscripts to read than normal, so rather than saving them for a train journey to London, I did the next best thing and took them on holiday with me. I was being rather hopeful that, in spite of trying to entertain two teenage daughters and keep my young niece and nephew happy, I would somehow be able to steal away the time to read them.

Under a windbreak bought hurriedly from Aldi—cheep and cheerful and just the thing to keep the sand from sheering our faces off—I took out my first manuscript and settled down. Captivated by its title—*To Honour God*—I reflected on the notion that there is a book in all of us. Few manage to accomplish writing it and, even among those who do, fewer manage to capture the essence and depth of its contents with a title as comprehensive and thought-provoking as this. The title represents a young man's struggle to live up to the very honourable name given to him at birth by his proud parents. As he grows out of 'the innocent faith of childhood' and into adulthood he has the compelling realisation that 'between my soul and God lie my heart and my deeds.' Pure intentions, the author resolutely points out—while ensuring that all actions and, more importantly, 'acts of worship are done exclusively for God's pleasure'—lie at the very heart of this profound truth.

In his accompanying email, the author suggested that the book was a collection of thoughts on his journey to Islam compiled primarily to bring consolation to members of his family who found the whole experience challenging, to say the least. I am not quite sure when I first had the pleasure of meeting the author, but I recall attending his wedding in one of London's most colourful and traditional places of worship, the Suleymaniye mosque in Shoreditch, in September 2001. Even more memorable was meeting his family and in particular his paternal grandmother who, in clearly expressing her affection and admiration for her beloved grandson, had travelled from the north of England to attend his marriage to a convert to Islam of Armenian origin. Though shy and retiring, Timothy was a gracious host. His character and personality leave a lasting and endearing impression on all who have enjoyed the sweetness of his company and hospitality.

Timothy sought my views on the manuscript before sending it to his family, explaining that it was not written for a wider audience, although it was hoped that its 'initial audience might come to understand my reasons for travelling this road'. This I could relate to. I imagine that most converts to Islam feel the need to explain comprehensively how it was that they embarked on the journey of faith and spirituality, and by doing so ease any tensions that have been aroused on both sides of the family divide. Some are wary of addressing the subject for fear of demolishing the fragile bridges that have been built, often painstakingly, but threaten to disintegrate every time there is an event which brings shame or disrepute on this great faith. Others have noble intentions of writing later in life for fear that issues of such magnitude are, for the time-being, just a little too close to the bone. The preferable alternative might be to wait until a certain maturity, perhaps lacking in the earlier stages of conversion, brings an ease that allows all that might have been aired then to now be expressed to an audience that has mellowed over the years. Others, for reasons known only to themselves, take the whole episode to their graves and, were it not for a book such as this, we would have little appreciation of how it was for them.

For those who have lived similar experiences—the anguish of the searching soul, the pain of setting oneself outside the family norms, the loneliness of that well-travelled yet eerily quiet road—reading this book will stir poignant memories that many might wish to forget. For others who have been attracted by the title, it will open the largely unexplored world of conversion and the inner search for faith—a search that is neither trifling nor for the faint hearted. It is not a typical story detailing *why I came to Islam*, interspersed with a few well-chosen verses from the Qur'an or *hadith*. It is a moving account of a young man's search for God set in the English and Scottish countryside, so full of manifestations of His Glory and Majesty, as well as on the well-trodden streets of London, making the account resonate with the concept of a British Islam.

Events that have taken place in the Muslim world and the United Kingdom and how they affected relationships with friends and family are explored, as are the affects of these events on the author's understanding of Islam as they frame the 'phases of realisation and renewal' which have been the 'central theme' of his profound religious experience and that of the community of Muslims with whom he is linked. How could his reading of a religion, which brought only peace and contentment to his heart, be interpreted in such a bizarre and warped manner by others? While seeking the middle ground, it sometimes feels as if one is going against those you love and who raised you to seek truth and justice wherever it is seen to be lacking; finding that 'belief in Islam is a continuation of upbringing and not a rejection of it' is a most valuable asset in that process.

The definitions of Britishness and the author's understanding of himself as being multi-cultural in lineage and in taking with him a part of the many places around the United Kingdom where he has worked, studied and holidayed are most insightful. And while examining the conflict of defining who we are in the game of *us* versus *them*, the bigger picture of gratitude to

God is articulately expressed: from the loving parents who nurtured and, with the help of that most stalwart of agencies, the Sunday school, provided the moral compass necessary to navigate through life, to gratitude to God that 'blessing after blessing has been bestowed' in spite of himself and his 'moments of sadness and ingratitude'.

When we choose to do things in secret—and let's face it, most converts have pursued the path of Islam in relative secrecy for a variety of reasons—it can be both frightening and fascinating. Frightening perhaps, for those around us who understand little of the journey we have embarked upon, much less the faith of Islam itself. It can also, however, be a fascinating experience and one that can enrich the lives of those who have the privilege of reading a well-documented account of the soul-searching experience that is finding one's path to God.

I felt fortunate, in spite of my damp holiday, for having been given the privilege of reading and drawing strength and comfort from another's story and, in doing so, reflecting on and drawing strength from my own.

Batool Al-Toma, Spring 2008
The New Muslims' Project
The Islamic Foundation

A Few Words About This Book

At the outset, I had no intention of publishing this work in the commercial sense. We live in an age in which books have come to be seen as commodities that are sold in units of thousands. This work, by contrast, was to have a print-run numbering a mere handful, for I had written it solely for my family and friends who remain puzzled by my adoption of Islam as the way by which I live my life. It was my part of a conversation, unheard amidst a hundred hypotheses about what had led me here.

Clearly something went awry with that intention, for my book now finds itself in the hands of strangers. For me there was no extravagance in writing so many words for so few to read or printing so few copies despite so much effort, but others were to disagree. I maintained my stance from the day I wrote the first word, throughout the writing process and into the final edits—and there appeared my foe: proofreaders! It is due to their persistent petitioning that I finally agreed to consider publishing this work for a wider audience.

Yet the consequences of my initial aim remain: this is the narrative of one individual concerning a personal journey of faith. I did not set out to represent Islam—as has become fashionable in the publishing industry of late—or to speak for the Muslims. I did not aim to set out a manifesto for the future of Islam in Britain, or to define the direction of this community. My only hope was that those reading it—that initial audience of mine—might come to understand my reasons for travelling this road.

It is true too that this text focuses almost exclusively on the interface between Islam and Christianity, as if these were the only two traditions that mattered. Awkward as this may be for readers without these traditions, it is again only a consequence of my reasons for creating this work. I know of no individual in my immediate or extended family who is not a practising Christian, while I count amongst them three priests, four former missionaries and numerous individuals involved in lay ministry. Similarly, this work is set within an English context, for I hail from this land. Some may feel that both these elements narrow my focus too much, but I believe there is little to be gained by my setting out to cover unfamiliar territory. The consequences of my initial aspirations remain.

Of the members of my family, it could be fairly said that I am the least pious. All attend church regularly and play an active role in their communions, whether inspiring others with their speech or delivering hot food to the homeless on cold winter nights. It is sometimes held that those who take up the mantle of faith anew become its true exemplars, but this is rarely the case. The prophets, our scriptures teach us, were sent to less than perfect individuals; the process of reform that follows the message is necessarily taxing and slow. The story I recount here, then, is no great sermon; at best, it is a series of reflections upon a journey.

I am naturally conscious of the need for greater understanding between communities, however: a realisation that dawned on me within a matter of weeks of my testimony of faith. In 1998 I was living in a flat owned by a Christian housing association in central London. As the summer term came to an end, my student neighbour moved out and was replaced by a middle-aged man whose faith in saving grace was strong. It was not long before he was inviting me to his church when we encountered one another in the kitchen. At first I would politely decline. Later I would give non-specific excuses for my refusals, but nothing I could say would satisfy him. Finally, when I could respond to his demands no more, I quietly told him that I had become Muslim just a month or two earlier. This revelation brought the invitations to a halt, but it appeared that they were just the start. Over the weeks that followed I was subjected to the most peculiar behaviour on the part of my flatmate. On several occasions he trailed the speakers from his record player out into the landing, placed them against my bedroom door and proceeded to blast me with Christian rock music for as long as he possibly could.

Others, in my position, would have written to the housing association to complain of harassment from a neighbour, but I—in apologetic fashion—sent a letter to my landlord explaining that since moving into the flat as a searching agnostic I had found my faith, but that such a faith was not Christianity, and that I was conscious that their organisation intended to serve Christians, and that I had noticed that one of my flatmates had taken exception to my faith and that he was uncomfortable living with me, and that I proposed to move out to placate him.

The initial response I received from my housing officer was kind, but I was about to encounter the unpleasant face of another. As I sat out my notice period, there was a break-in downstairs; an intruder had failed to access a bedroom via the normal route and had hacked through the plasterboard wall instead. The tenant was naturally shaken by the incident, as we all were. The residents of the downstairs flat had just realised that leaving a window accessible to neighbouring buildings wide open in one of the most crime ridden parts of central London was hardly wise. Yet the drug addicts and dealers for which the area was notorious were not the prime suspects.

While I was preparing to set off for the library one morning, I received a telephone call from the housing association. It was not the officer I was used to dealing with and we exchanged none of the usual pleasantries. Taking up my letter to her colleague, she noted my new found faith and, almost in the same breath, asked if I had anything to do with the break-in downstairs. I was mortified. As her accusing words rang in my ears—'It's disgusting!'—I wondered how I had transformed from the 'nice', 'quiet' tenant who had been praised for cleaning the flats each week to one capable of attempting to enter another's room by merciless force. How was it that my desire to honour God had been ripped to shreds and twisted into the pursuit of criminality?

If ever there was evidence for the need for greater understanding between communities, it was here. Unfortunately, the chasm of mutual incomprehension is vast and a hundred other cases like mine could easily be recounted to illustrate as much. While I insisted on keeping to my plan of publishing just a few copies of this work, it was largely this issue that led others to ask me to reconsider. If, therefore, this work can lead to greater understanding in some small way, *Alhamdulilah*—all praise is for God—*Hallelujah!*

The proofreaders have spoken and so I pray there may be benefit in this work for others.

Timothy Bowes, Spring 2008
Chesham, England

Shukr

Here I would like to express my gratitude. First of all, to my Creator without Whom nothing would be possible. It is only by His generosity that I have achieved anything at all. He knows my prayer better than I do—He is with you wherever you are, says the Qur'an—and so this eulogy continues off the page.

A well-known *hadith*, meanwhile, tells us that the Prophet ﷺ said: 'He who does not thank people, does not thank God.' There are many who helped in the preparation of this work, all of whom have my prayers, but there are a few I would like to mention by name: Abdulbaasit Kazmi, Aaminah Hernández, Batool Al-Toma, Hillary Saunders, Mohamed Hassani and, of course, my beloved wife, Zeynep. *Jazaak Allahu khayran!*

My thanks would be incomplete without mention of my parents, whose years of sermon writing made me appreciate parables in all that surrounds me.

> *'My Lord, bestow on them Your mercy
> even as they cherished me in childhood.'*

Qur'an 17:24

I am very grateful for their constant giving throughout my life. To them and all who have helped and supported me: thank you.

CHAPTER ONE

Reconciling the Heart

Between my soul and God lie my heart and my deeds. Nothing else lies between us. It is 16 years since I departed from the religious tradition of my family. Although I was confirmed into the Anglican Communion on Sunday, 2 December, 1990, by Bishop James Jones, my faith was already wavering. Within two years, the doubt outweighed my faith: the doubts within my faith gave way to religious agnosticism, which in turn gave way to atheism. In time, belief in God returned, but belief that a man was God never did. I became a searching agnostic, one who sought truth. I did not know where this quest would lead until I arrived at the destination—and it was only a hesitation within the journey, not its termination, for my pursuit goes on. When I came to believe in Islam in 1998 it was not the end of the road, but merely a stopping point along the way.

By its very nature, agnosticism need not cause particular problems in the relationship between people, even if it is disliked. The agnostic has no commitments to observe, other than the call of his heart regarding sincerity. Thus he may attend family gatherings with ease, his presence never an intrusion. In the case of one who adopts another faith the situation is quite different: he has rites and principles he must observe which create differences. I have experienced both scenarios and I am acutely aware which is the more problematic.

It is impossible to ignore the fact that my belief in Islam causes deep unhappiness within my family. Despite suggestions to the contrary, this is a reality I have never denied. Yet doubt is cast on this claim of mine, for I apparently continue to cling stubbornly to my principles. Is this not evidence enough that I am unaware of the impact of my beliefs?

The answer is no. I am acutely aware of the feelings of those around me, but matters of faith—and of the heart—require action. While I am not a good believer and my practice is hugely wanting, I do believe sincerely. My faith is not something that I take lightly, nor one that I took on as a choice of fashion. I came down this path because I believe it to be the best way to worship God. For this reason, I cannot turn my back on it just to bring ease in my personal relationships.

The heart and our deeds are all that lie between us and our Creator. Only two know what is in our hearts and they are God and ourselves. Faith or doubt, love or malice, sincerity or hypocrisy: these are known to us and to God alone. For me, the one aspect that recurred time and again was sincerity versus hypocrisy. It was this that forced me to sit at the back of the church and to utter only a few lines of the *Nicene Creed* for more than two years. It was this issue that made the question of faith seem so difficult as I engaged in my search for truth. In 1997 I was continually writing about the matter, much to the distaste of friends whose rational minds had long since abandoned belief in God. The following reflects my feelings at the time:

> You don't want to reject their faith, you don't want to be different, you don't want to be an outcast; you just don't have their faith, but at least you're trying to find it. But it's so hard to admit that. They prefer to hear that you're lazy, because that's not such a disgrace. You're filled with fear, so you don't admit openly that you're completely lost. You're hoping that someone will pick up on your blatant hints.

Halfway through my first degree, I found myself with an intense thirst to find my way in faith. On the one hand I wanted to believe like every other member of my family, on the other, I was adamant that sincerity before God was paramount. Thus that same piece went on:

> I can listen to the readings, the gospel and a psalm. I can listen to the sermon and learn. But how do you think I feel when we all stand for the *Nicene Creed*, and all I can say is 'I believe in one God the father almighty, maker of Heaven and Earth, and of all things visible and invisible'? You want me to say it all, but faith isn't about you, it's about God. Do you want me to be a hypocrite before God? Of course you don't. I don't go to church because I don't have the strength or the knowledge to claim your faith and I refuse to lie in the Name of God.

Later on, having learnt something of Islam, I expressed similar concerns. I recently came across an old notebook into which I had poured my thoughts as my interest in the Muslim faith grew. Penned over two sides of lined paper, I found a lengthy answer to a question somebody must have asked me around that time. I had obviously said that I could never be a Muslim and had thus written a series of paragraphs under four headings to explain why: the hypocrite; knowledge of one's self; true belief; and fear of rejection. Each passage focused on a matter that troubled me within. Of true belief I wrote:

> I must believe: truly and truthfully. Of course I believe in God, our Creator, but the faith through which I should worship Him is still unclear to me. I refuse to have a blind faith; this is obvious, for would I have gone astray otherwise? To be convinced by man of the right path is not enough. The proof should be in the religion itself.

A fellow student—hearing my complaints about my lack of faith—once told me: 'The problem with you is that you question it; I'd never question it.' I was never able to accept this view, for I felt that it was important to be able to say what I believe with conviction. I was one who would say, 'I'm not really sure, I'm confused, I'm lost,' in contrast to the person who could simply say, 'I don't have a reason, I just believe it—it's just my religion.' The source of this lies in the heart.

The journey of the heart is ongoing and continuous. Though those early obsessions have subsided, the question of reconciling my heart goes on. Between my soul and God, I remind myself over and over again, lie my heart and my deeds. I no longer have the luxury of the simple and innocent faith of childhood.

In the Islamic tradition, the child is considered pure—there is no concept of original sin, and the child that dies in infancy will go straight to paradise—but we do not need faith to tell us this. The pleasing faith of the child makes this self-evident. Contrast its simplicity to the perplexity of adolescence; in my case, the two do not compare: my earliest days were characterised by my taking key principles to heart. In primary school I would censure friends who exclaimed, 'Oh my God,' for one of my godparents had criticised those who took the Lord's name in vain. In junior school I refused to provide a cover story for a friend in trouble because I believed that as a Christian I could not lie. Later on, when I was asked why I did not stand up to a boy who was picking on me on the bus on my way home from school, I got the first inkling that something was amiss in my simplistic interpretation of the command to turn the other cheek.

Blessed are the little ones, say the scriptures of more than one tradition. My wife and I once looked on in awe as a tiny baby, with eyes closed, lay in a cot before us and raised her miniature hands out in front of her, cupping them just like our own as we prayed for her, her parents and ourselves. We all knew who the best amongst us was. A few days later we received news that this baby, born prematurely, had also left us prematurely. Blessed are the little ones: a friend of the grieving father reminded him that these children are the residents of Paradise. Of these children on the Day of Judgement, our Prophet ﷺ said: 'They will meet their parents and grab them by their garments or their hands to no end other than that God will enter them into Paradise.'[1]

As we grow older we cloud matters with prejudice and desire, losing sight of the pure and beautiful. Certainly, in time, the church I attended in early childhood became the target of derision although it had been responsible for promoting ideas of good living amongst its congregation. Its leader was sometimes unflatteringly described as a fanatic, and yet he taught us to thank the Lord for the blessings He bestowed upon us week after week and that our faith was one that brought joy, that we should wear like a garment and not be ashamed of sharing. Yet, for some, our family's move from a more charismatic, evangelical church to a traditional Anglican place of worship was a cause for celebration.

Looking back on that transition, however, I wonder whether my later hesitation in faith was a result of swapping dogmatism for something a little vague. As I got older, I found myself less keen on revealing my faith to friends, shying away from exhibiting overtly Christian behaviour. Indeed, just 19 hours after I was confirmed into the Anglican Communion, I cringed with embarrassment when a friend from church congratulated me in front of my classmates at school.

It was during a Christian holiday camp which took me away from home and my family for a week that I found myself clearly conscious of the fragility of my faith. My companions at the Lakeside YMCA centre in Windermere, whom I had never met before, were characterised by their zeal. Their style of worship reminded me of my early church. On the first evening, witnessing their enthusiastic worship in a marquee on the site, I found myself uncomfortable in their company. This was partly because I was a rather shy character and partly because I had grown used to the more reserved, restrained worship of our traditional church. Yet there was another cause of my discomfort: the recognition that I did not have the strength of faith that would allow me to sing those songs with such cheer and dedication. It was a feeling that began to recur.

Over two or three consecutive summers I journeyed to the small Hebridean island of Iona, a mile from the shores of Mull, its sights and sounds pulling me back. I could walk from one end to the other in an afternoon, three miles from a white, sandy beach to a dark, grey cliff top—and from time to time I still find myself traversing those paths in my dreams. My first visit was with a small group of young Christians from the Dioceses of York, although we soon became attached to a larger group from across Europe travelling in the same direction. Catching the early train at York, we headed north into Scotland and on up to Glasgow Queen Street station in time to catch the midday train to Oban. The winding journey along the base of vast, dark green valleys was painfully slow, but somehow it aroused my curiosity: there was something unique about this expedition, I thought. Its ease unapparent, there was a definite sense of journey. We arrived in Oban three hours later. From there, the voyage by ferry around the islands took three-quarters of an hour, docking at Craignure on the Isle of Mull. We travelled on by coach, cross country to Fionnphort, another journey lasting two hours. The last, and welcome, leg was the ferry to Iona itself, which turned out to be a pleasantly brief crossing.

Wearied, but relieved, we reached the MacLeod Centre on the lower slopes of a hill beyond the Benedictine Abbey in the early evening. Separating from my Yorkshire companions, I found myself sharing a room with characters from across the continent, one of whom stood out immediately. His feet shod in sandals and his scalp hidden beneath a wide-brimmed straw hat, this blond-bearded German soon took to playing *House of the Rising Sun* on his acoustic guitar over and over again.

For the next week I would be a visiting member of the Iona Community, which was founded in 1938 by Reverend George McLeod on the site of a much earlier Christian community. It is believed that Columba—a Catholic saint who had previously established a number of monasteries in Ireland—set down on one of the island's shores around 563CE. Having led an army in battle at home that left 3,000 men dead, he had fled Ireland with 12 others, intent on seeking refuge on the west coast of Scotland. His exile may have been an attempt to escape his conscience as much as retribution. When he finally arrived on Iona by coracle, it was to change the destiny of this small, exposed outcrop amidst choppy seas; he climbed to the summit of its highest hill and looked across the horizon. Standing atop Carn-Cul-ri-Eirinn—the hill with its back to Ireland—he could no longer see his homeland, and Iona became his home.

The modern community is centred upon a 10th-century abbey which post-dated the monastery that Columba built, but its spiritual essence undoubtedly has different ancestry. Although its current incarnation started as a project linked to the Church of Scotland, it is now an ecumenical community which appeals to Christians of many denominations and of different social and cultural backgrounds. Its liberal approach brings together individuals who are interested in restoring the common life through social and political works, empathising with issues of peace and justice. It was the emphasis on social work that appealed to me more than the call to renew a faith based on the gospels, and it was this that drew me back the following year.

The MacLeod Centre was a modern building accommodating arts facilities, meeting rooms, a kitchen and dining room, a social area and numerous bedrooms. We soon learnt that we were there to live as a cooperative community for the week, each of us given our chores. On one day we would be cleaning the toilets, on another doing the washing up or clearing the breakfast tables. The water we drank was coloured by the peat on the moor, dribbling out of the taps straight from the island's own reservoir. Our food came from the community's allotments. Living as companions from several nations was relatively simple.

Given that the activities we engaged in were challenging, we always thought deeply about the issues raised. Meanwhile, Iona's unique liturgy used in worship every day was intensely moving, pulling unexpected emotions out from the depths of our souls. The mid-week pilgrimage around the island focused on its history and provided pause for reflection. Entering this environment as one whose faith was doubtful, however, generated its own set of emotions, leaving me confused and feeling lost. Conscious of the weakness of my faith, I demanded the signs that those early saints were said to have witnessed on the island. If old sages had seen Christ before them on these rocks, why could he not reveal himself to me?

While I had travelled to Iona in a group, I soon found that I preferred solitude. Our mornings and evenings were spent in workshops, but our afternoons were free and so I would wander off to explore the lanes and footpaths on my own. Every evening a beautiful service was held in the abbey, but I soon found myself uncomfortable within those stone walls, mindful of my weak faith and the resulting sense of hypocrisy that dominated me.

By the middle of the week, I was no longer hurrying down to the abbey for worship before sunset, but heading off in the opposite direction, climbing the steep hillside to the summit of Dún-I, where I would sit at the base of a huge rock and survey the scene below me. I would stay there until I saw people—the like of ants from that height—emerge from the abbey's entrance and then I would descend the slopes again while there was still light, the sky already orange, to meet my companions in the MacLeod Centre in time for our evening activities.

One evening towards the end of the week I took part in a workshop in which we were asked to ponder upon what we possessed, whether that was something tangible, a relationship, a collection of material goods or something of emotional value. Unfortunately, despite the many very real blessings I had been bestowed with—my family, my home, my education—I was an unhappy, pessimistic teenager. The purpose of the workshop had been to link what we had been given in life to the existence of a generous God, so that we might find greater focus in our worship, expressing real gratitude in prayer. When my depression broke this linkage, however, my fragile faith evolved into disbelief and I now denied that we had a Creator and an Overseer of our affairs.

That same evening I climbed half way up Dún-I again and stood looking up towards the stars. I drove myself to tears and in a moment's theatre cried out, 'You're not real, you're not there'—an irony that was lost on me at the time. It was an act of rebellion at first more than an affirmation of a reality that had dawned on me just then. My faith was weak to be sure, but I was no more convinced by my disbelief than I was by the belief which had accompanied me throughout my childhood. Yet just as faith can grow over time, my belief in nothingness became almost religious as I served it with the philosophical acrobatics of an immature mind.

I confessed my unbelief to my mother on my return from Iona, half hoping that she would have words to convince me that our faith was true and half hoping that she would accept the conclusion I had reached. It had never occurred to me that I was not alone in my struggle to find faith and so it came as some surprise that one of my brothers had found the writings of the Archbishop of Durham useful in setting him back on track. Instead of feeling reassured, however, I just found myself more confused.

Initially disbelief gave rise to questions about the meaning of life and the nature of the universe. I used to wonder whether the nothingness on the outside of the universe—if such a place existed—was of the same substance as the nothingness between all the matter contained within it.

I used to wonder if every star above us at night was a clone of our galaxy, each following an identical course but in the future and the past. I used to wonder how it had all started and how, given the infinite timescale involved, we had ever reached today. I pondered on questions that my mind was too small to comprehend, until at last I absorbed myself in science fiction and settled for the make-believe world of time travel and quantum leaps.

If I could not convince my family that I was too tired to attend church on a Sunday morning, I would insist on sitting at the back only to observe. This was not a boycott of my family: my brothers were already away from home and studying at university, my sister was in the choir, my father was invariably involved in lay preaching and my mother in delivering the sacraments. At the communion rail, I would hide my hands and bow my head, seeking only the blessing and refusing the bread and wine. Instead of singing hymns I would gulp like a fish, opening and closing my lips silently with my hymnal in hand, declining to read those words.

Although I claimed not to believe in God, those actions spawned by the feeling of hypocrisy revealed a subconscious faith. I might well have argued that my concern was discomfort at that stage, asserting that as an autonomous character, nobody knew what my heart contained except me, but my behaviour consistently proved otherwise. Nevertheless, there is no denying that such discomfort was sometimes unbearably painful.

The death of a loved one when you believe in nothingness, when you believe that life has no meaning and that this life is all there is—death when you do not believe—is an emotionally crushing experience. When my maternal grandfather passed away, clearly every member of our family was terribly upset. Yet his funeral was marked out by the sense of optimism which pervaded it, the service really quite beautiful and profound. My grandfather was an ever-generous gentleman who lived a good life all of his years. In that country setting in the heart of Buckinghamshire, on a lovely summer's day, there was a sense of peace. The message that day was clear. There was upset, but not grief, because the faithful saw that, as a deeply kind, practising Christian, he was taking his place in Paradise. As for this 16-year-old boy: disbelieving in God, and therefore in the Day of Judgement and the Hereafter, I could not come to terms with this. My grief overwhelmed me and I could find no solace in the words of all those compassionate souls surrounding me. I felt all alone and I began to see greater meanings in those initial meanderings of my mind than I could have intended at the time: nothingness amidst nothingness.

Doubt, however, does not only apply to belief, but to disbelief as well. As much as I rejected belief, I was also becoming agnostic in my atheism. A change of scenery confirmed this when, in 1996, quite apprehensive about a journey across a continent, I travelled to Tanzania in east Africa. When my plane touched down in Darussalam on a very warm winter's evening there was some sense of relief. Sweating in the unexpected heat, I was greeted affectionately in the airport lobby by my uncle and aunt who were clearly happy to see me. That night we slept in the Catholic Secretariat beneath mosquito nets, the song of insects outside cheering my arrival.

Darussalam was bustling on Sunday morning, a scene far removed from the sleepy Sabbath days of suburban England. Warm conversation greeted our arrival in town, a Tanzanian at the telephone kiosk engaging my aunt with Swahili chit-chat. After a telephone call home, we were soon on the road again, heading out of the coastal city in my uncle's white Land Rover. All along the edge of the potholed Tarmac road, salesmen could be seen selling every conceivable ware: bananas, bricks, Coca-Cola, clothes. Into the countryside, their numbers lessened, the stalls replaced by fields, homes and forest. Out here the vegetation was lush and green, revealing banana palms, coconut palms and even rice on the low river-fed fields.

We stopped for lunch in Morogoro at the New Green Restaurant, 2,000 feet above sea level. Though there was a short rain shower during our stopover, the vegetation was not as fresh here as it had been towards the coast. The journey onwards was long, for we were heading far into the interior where the land was dry, the earth dusty and the plants pale in colour, but the smooth road afforded us some comfort. To our left and right, graceful mountains rose out of the plain, each one veiled beneath a layer of trees. Forty kilometres from our destination, we finally cut off the good road and took to a dirt track across Kongwa Ranch, passing through Kongwa town and then the village between it and St Philip's Theological College. After a full day travelling, we arrived at our destination at six in the evening.

The Iona community—in whose company I had lost my faith—out in the Sea of the Hebrides thousands of miles from here was famous for its African choruses: I used to love those atmospheric gatherings in the abbey. Yet those Celtic renderings of Swahili and Zulu verse paled now as the native voices rose into the heavens from the evening service in the white-walled chapel. Those songs were my welcome to this college in the heart of Tanzania. I loved my hosts' flat at the head of the road: its views were spectacular, while its architectural style appealed to me. I slept well that first night on the campus.

The following day was a national holiday in honour of 500 people—many of them students returning home following their exams—who had died in the *MV Bukoba* ferry disaster on Lake Victoria a month earlier. All around there was a sense of mourning. It was a sad day, but at the time I considered it a blessing in a way: it gave me pause to reflect on my own approach to death. It seemed to me that death was not a taboo as it often seemed to be within my own culture, two years before the very public outpouring of grief that marked the passing of a princess: a taboo which seemed to leave behind so much pain as the consequences of loss and sorrow were hidden away. I wondered whether the source of this was a greater appreciation of life and death. In the afternoon, a service was held in memory of the mother of one of the college workers, who had just died from tuberculosis. In England in our era, I thought, we do not know of TB, polio or pandemic flu and the survival rate among children is good: and so death is perceived differently, I believed. As the departed soul was remembered in the chapel, beautiful African hymns were drifting through the air once more.

Despite my own shyness, everyone I met seemed to be extremely friendly and kind. A young man called Yohana brought me his school exercise book one evening in an effort to help me grasp his Swahili tongue. Everyone I met on a personal level was welcoming and yet that paranoid discomfort remained. Travelling up to the capital, I interpreted faces and eyes in my own way, worrying about those glances from strangers. Dodoma was hot and dusty, its climate distinct from coastal Darussalam, just like Ankara compared to Istanbul. My uncle was visiting the bishops at the cathedral and so I spent the day wandering around the town with my aunt. In that suffocating heat, a chilled bottle of ginger beer was most welcome, but it did not set my mind at ease. I was a self-conscious visitor to that unfamiliar country in 1996. I was anxious about the European colonial past and about how I would be perceived in that now independent land. What was I to make of the glances of the people I passed by? These were amongst my thoughts throughout my stay as a white-faced guest in a proud African state, even after I came across the following advice in my Swahili textbook:

> In Tanzanian culture there are conventions about who is the first to speak. It is usually the person of lower status who greets the other person. A stranger entering a village should greet the villagers who will then welcome him. These are conventions that should be noted, for the visitor will feel unwanted because nobody speaks and everyone looks unwelcoming, likewise the villagers may misinterpret it and feel offended because he is wandering around in their territory without even having the decency to make himself known to them. It is important in Swahili culture to greet people properly. A smile or a mumbled word is not sufficient and it is considered rude to ignore people.[2]

This discovery proved to be a valuable lesson for the years that followed, as I navigated my way between various unfamiliar cultures. Many a misunderstanding can be avoided by replacing assumption with learning. In Tanzania, for every encounter with strangers and my perception of it, my meeting with individuals seemed to throw doubt on my previous conclusions. Tuesday, 18 June, was a day of conversation, surprising me given my frequent reversion to silence. From next door came the Rwandan sisters, intent on bringing more Swahili through my lips, for my lack of words was quite an aberration in this land. After lunch I ventured down the road to the student accommodation closer to the chapel where I met three trainee priests: Amon, Suleman and Mote. Mote had excellent English and thus acted as an interpreter between the others and myself: Suleman explained that they had been expecting me to visit and that not visiting would usually be interpreted as a sign of hostility. Taking his obvious upset to heart, I found myself visiting almost every day after that.

One evening, a very sick child was brought to my aunt as the doctor on the campus. Tending to the frail girl in her mother's arms, she gave her some kind of injection. It struck me as a strong reminder of how fragile life is and how precious people are. The previous night the father of one of the night watchmen had died of illness and now there was this sight of a hopelessly weak child. All I could do was pray. I did not know what the illness was, or how serious it was, but the concern that I saw in my aunt's face after the family left told me that this was a delicate situation. I felt sad realising that this family was lucky in being able to see a doctor and I wondered how many other families would go without healthcare at a time like this.

That night I prayed, seeking the aid of our Creator. As an agnostic without the strong faith of my family it was something that did not come from me easily, but the sight of that poor girl prompted me to take the only action that was within my grasp. With genuine concern and true sincerity, I prayed in the darkness until I was too tired, begging for an answer well into the night, asking that the girl would be blessed and return to health.

Were my prayers answered or was it just the *dawa*, I asked the following day? I did not know, but hearing news of her recovery,

I decided not to reject my initial reaction: that someone up there had listened to me. I did not know if I should read unnatural causes into what I encountered, but sometimes I believed strongly that there was something guiding me. I found myself in the heart of Tanzania with a group of theological students who, despite myself, had offered me great friendship. I found myself listening to their beautiful choruses and gripped by discussions about how the church should act in our world. At the time, I thought that I might be searching all my life for faith, but just then I decided that I would not give up. The previous day I had seen a vomiting, dehydrated child. Today she was looking so much better and was eating at last. I wanted to praise the Lord for that.

It is difficult to recall the journey between faith, disbelief and agnosticism in any detail, for the latter two are characterised by feelings rather than action. Nevertheless, the signposts remain. I do not remember when my belief in God returned, but I do know that for a long time I would utter only a portion of the *Nicene Creed*: 'I believe in one God, creator of Heaven and Earth.' For the most part, from the point of my rejection of belief, I did believe in God—only occasionally did I find myself without any faith at all—but I never regained the belief that Jesus ﷺ was God. While many people talk of not understanding the Trinity, my problem was much more elemental; I had no deep philosophical objection, only a strong feeling inside that God was completely separate from His creation.

It was as my first year at university drew to a close that I began to feel the need to find truth. During the summer holidays I attended a service at London's All Souls Langham Place with my maternal grandmother where I listened to a sermon which impressed me, inspiring me to reform myself. With the start of the new term I began attending All Souls every Sunday just to listen to the sermon—and perhaps to get a good lunch. My weekly trek from King's Cross to Regent Street lasted for about two months, only for it to end abruptly. On my final visit, the evangelical preacher invited all those who

were still unsure about his message to stay behind after the
service for whom he promised a clearer explanation. Since that
was my very reason for attending, I decided to accept his
invitation and waited in the church beside a kind, elderly
couple. His advice, however, angered me, for it was a lazy
explanation, poorly thought through for an agnostic audience
such as this and I decided not to return the following week.

At university I had disassociated myself from many of those I
had known the previous term and kept myself to myself. I felt
that I had been unduly influenced by friends into behaving
foolishly in my first year and now found myself seeking to
escape that way of life. But for the company of a friend of mine
who was interested in Islam although she was not Muslim, I
became quite a recluse and would not even go to sit in the pub,
preferring instead to seek out new corners of the library and
wander the greener parts of London. As the academic year
progressed I became obsessed with my search for faith. Although
I knew very few Muslims other than those with whom I had
come into conflict during the course of the previous year, I
started to read into Islam, impressed by the manners of one
student I had never spoken to, the content of books in the library
and the general enthusiasm of my non-Muslim friend for this
alien culture. Gradually I began to appreciate this unknown
faith. I found myself contemplating two traditions—sometimes
simultaneously, sometimes in turns—negotiating my path back
towards God ﷻ.

Two Traditions

Over the years, I have encountered a small number of Muslims who used to be priests, preachers or other members of the church. There was the former Roman Catholic priest who headed off to work in Egypt; the former nun who now dedicates herself to looking after her disabled son; the bishop of the Catholic Apostolic Church; the former Methodist minister who rediscovered Jesus the Son of Man in Islam; and the teacher of religious education who adopted the faith just before he completed his training to be an Anglican priest and without ever meeting a Muslim. On every occasion, I am reminded of what the two traditions hold in common, rather than what separates them.

This recognition emerges as soon as these converts open their mouths to speak. If I close my eyes, I can picture them wearing a clerical collar, not because I know what they used to do, but due to their manner of speech. I popped into a mosque one Saturday afternoon to do my midday prayer after a day out in London and decided to wander downstairs to catch the last half of a talk in the meeting room. As soon as I sat down I was sent back in time and found myself listening to a friendly, charismatic vicar—except that the theology and terminology was Islamic. I realised that the gulf between the two traditions is not as great as we sometimes think it is.

I once knew a fellow who explained that the reason he was not taking his shoes off to pray on the dusty carpet in the basement of his bookshop was that we should differentiate ourselves from the Jews and the Christians. I had heard other justifications for shoes-on-carpet before, but I thought he was confused. I pointed out that, in this country certainly, Christians do not tend to take their shoes off when they go to church; at home too, often they do not remove them at the door. Far from differentiating himself from the Jews and Christians, he was differentiating himself from others quite like him.

Pondering the legacy of my Christian upbringing, those sometimes argumentative discussions seem quite strange now. The initial response of one who adopts a new faith—even the latent Catholic who finds himself a sudden evangelist—is often to reject all that passed before. Yet when I think about the trend of rejection more deeply, it seems obvious that I should question how much of it is just skin deep.

Much of who I am, how I act and what I think are a legacy of my Christian education. This upbringing taught me good manners and modesty, both of which are perfectly admirable Islamic characteristics. Concerns about global justice and social responsibility spring from this root as well. As a Muslim who believes that fairness and social work is part of my religion, I buy Fairtrade products, but I still acknowledge the root of this concern. I buy my meat from a smallholder in Somerset and sometimes my milk direct from the producing farm. All of this is a legacy of my upbringing.

Yet my background has done more than affect how I act: it can be seen in my thinking. As a Christian I was raised on the parables and reported stories of Jesus' ﷻ life in the four gospels. The commentary provided by Paul's epistles seemed less important in childhood than for the adult faithful. Jesus' ﷻ exhortations to the Pharisees to observe the spirit of the Law is no doubt reflected throughout everything I write. Although Luke tells us of a dream in which all foods were shown to be lawful in his *Acts of the Apostles*, the gospel accounts appear to call for an appreciation of the purpose of the Law, not its rejection. Unconsciously I see this affecting the way I live, although this is not to deny the impact of other aspects of one's background on thought and belief. The society in which we are brought up, the education system and the impact of the media all affect our outlook. Some aspects that I am acutely aware of include cynicism, scepticism and suspicion. There is a degree to which these mores can be healthy, but they can also affect one negatively. In my case, I cannot watch recorded debates between Muslims and Christians, for example, because I find myself disputing the claims of both parties.

Our cultural background also affects how we look at the world around us. Societal norms, for example, make us look differently at our environment to how our predecessors did. I am very much aware that the way I think and act is far removed from the ways of those who passed before us. I have been conditioned by my environment to the extent that things once viewed as extremes are now the norm and things once seen as normal are now considered wild aberrations.

The overwhelming feeling, however, is not to consider Islam a negation of my upbringing, but rather a continuation of it. Indeed, retaining that which is good, I often consider it to be a perfection of my culture. There is no doubt that it is useful to acknowledge the legacy of our upbringing and to be truthful about this too, recognising that much in the trend of rejection that we encounter between individuals and nations is often very superficial.

The Creator

At the heart of our faith, whether we are Christian or Muslim, stands God, the Creator of all things. Unfortunately there exists a tendency in Britain to conflate ethnicity and religious identity, which leads to confusion as to what it is that the followers of Islam worship; some confuse us with Hindus, since the majority of Muslims in this country hail from South Asia. When clarifying what he meant by his use of the term 'Islams' one individual found that the description of the Hindu elephant god Ganesha best marked out the group of people he had in mind. When talking about the beliefs of Muslims, it is quite common to hear people refer to Allah ﷻ as if He were some handmade deity quite separate from what we conventionally refer to as God. For the Muslim who has in mind the One who created all things, this level of ignorance is quite perturbing. Allah is simply a proper noun in the Arabic language used to describe what English speakers refer to as God:

> Allah! There is no god but He—the Ever-Living, the Sustainer of all existence. Neither drowsiness overtakes Him, nor sleep. To Him belongs whatever is in the heavens and whatever is on the earth. Who is it that can intercede with Him except by His permission? He knows what is presently before them and what will be after them, and they encompass not a thing of His knowledge except for what He wills. His throne extends over the heavens and the earth, and their preservation tires Him not. And He is the Most High, the Most Great.[3]

We would not say that because French speakers use the word *Dieu*, or Spanish speakers *Dios*, that they worshipped a different god; the same is true of the Hebrew names *YHWH* and *Elohim*. The word Allah is used by Arabic-speaking Jews and Christians as well as Muslims and appears in Arabic translations of the Bible. Indeed, a Turkish copy of the gospels on my bookshelf uses the word Allah consistently throughout.

It is not language that separates us, but theology. While we may agree that our Creator is the central object of our devotion and worship, our descriptions of God inevitably lead us to reject the other's. One cannot believe that God is both a perichoresis of three persons and completely separate from His creation at the same time; the two approaches are incompatible, which naturally leads us to the conclusion that we worship different gods even if we agree that the focus of our devotion is our Creator. Orthodox Christianity and Islam are both defined by their clear and uncompromising descriptions of God, each presenting an obstacle to the other. The Trinity and *tawhid* appear to be at opposite ends of the spectrum. If this is a problem, it need not be. The request for understanding is not a demand for the other to believe as we do: merely a simple plea for honesty.

There were more than five years of agnosticism before I reaffirmed my belief in God with the faith of a believer. Looking back it seems ironic that the first thing I did after rejecting belief on my return from Iona was to start pondering what the universe was all about, for today it is its beauty and its expanse through space and time that strengthens my faith in God. A common refrain of the Muslim is *Allahu Akbar*—God is great—the meaning of which seems to be perfectly clear once we understand what He has done.

According to contemporary scientists, the universe probably came into being around 13.7 billion years ago. High energy physics has been used to describe the evolution of the universe in the period that followed, explaining how the first protons, electrons and neutrons formed. Scientists talk of the formation of the first nuclei, then the formation of atoms and of neutral hydrogen. A third period describes the formation of structure: matter coming together to form stars, quasars, galaxies, galaxy clusters and super clusters.

Some of the most beautiful images that I hold dear are those showing deep space as observed via the Hubble Space Telescope. Those images always warm my soul, reminding me of the grandeur of our Creator, putting everything into perspective. One of the most exciting developments of recent times was the Hubble Ultra Deep Field image, which was derived from data accumulated over a few months in 2003 and 2004. Although this has been described as covering a small region of space, it is estimated to contain 10,000 galaxies. As the deepest image of the universe ever taken using the visible spectrum, it takes us back in time more than 13 billion years, showing us how the universe looked in the early Stelliferous age.

While the images of deep space in themselves are always heart-warming, their significance is also profoundly felt when one considers the words of the Qur'an about God's creation. One verse fails to provide us with a woolly, open description that the post-enlightenment age has taught us to expect from scripture. Far from it: Hubble's image of the Eagle Nebula M16 could be used to illustrate this verse, which the non-Muslim, Arthur J Arberry, translated as follows in 1964:

> Then He lifted Himself to heaven when it was smoke, and said to it and to the earth, 'Come willingly, or unwillingly!' They said, 'We come willingly.'[4]

This need not come as a surprise for the Muslim who believes that the Qur'an is the Word of God. Of course the Creator can describe His creation in truthful terms. From His throne, He is witness to all things. For the disbeliever who considers the Qur'an to be the 1,400-year-old work of man, however, it is something to marvel: it would even be so had it originated in 1964, twenty-nine years before Hubble was operational. Surely God is magnificent.

For me, the sight of deep space or simply the stars above me on a dark night is a reminder of what we really mean when we say God is great. Indeed in these days of conflict it is necessary to remind ourselves of these things; if we set our short lives beside the 14 billion years of God's creation that we are aware of, it helps put everything into perspective, reminding us of our place. It reminds us why we are here and our part in the great scheme of things. That same Arabist translated another verse:

> Have not the unbelievers then beheld that the heavens and the earth were a mass all sewn up, then We unstitched them and of water fashioned every living thing? Will they not believe?[5]

Yes, I believe: God is truly magnificent. In reality, of course, we need not rely on high technology to witness the signs of creation. The signs of God surround us. Whether in the rolling forested hills of Dorking or in the sheets of coal mined from deep underground, His creation is awe-inspiring. The evolutionary process discerned in the creation of a coal field pales into insignificance when we begin to consider our own existence. We have travelled far from the formation of the first amino acids that scientists believe were polymerised billions of years ago to where we are today, with complex systems that provide us with sight, smell, taste and touch.[6] 'Or were they created from nothing,' asks the Qur'an, 'Or did they create themselves? Or were they the creators of the heavens and the earth? Nay! They have no certain knowledge.'[7]

The signs are self-evident in our creation, but they also reveal themselves throughout the passage of our lives. Some years back I was told that I could never have children of my own, the news broken by a locum doctor while my GP was on her summer holidays. Dealing with the sudden emotional burden, we cancelled our own travels that August and shed plenty of tears between us. Sometimes we would sit and read scriptures, making the supplications of Zachariah ﷺ who cried to his Lord for a child until He answered that prayer. As time went by, however, I began to come to terms with this news and accept it as the absolute truth; while my wife prayed for a child daily, my prayer became occasional, for the doctors had convinced me of its futility despite my knowledge that He who created me only needs to say 'Be' for new life to emerge. Every time my old friends from university announced that they were now parents, my mind told me to be happy, but instead I felt sad. With every visit from my niece I had to hold back tears.

It was pain like mourning; like losing someone. It was a loss, but others did not seem to understand, driving life on as normal. It was the pain of knowing that you have reached the end of the line, that you will be an ancestor for no one, that you will never have grandchildren who will ask you about your youth. Even if my family worried that I would raise my children in accordance with my faith, not theirs, it was a dream of mine that they could trace their Muslim ancestry, that the English Muslim would not forever be viewed as the queer aberration that comes and goes with every conversion and death. Instead there was this pain.

Not long before we received this news I had a dream one night which troubled me. My wife often has what I would call spiritual dreams, but mine are mostly non-descript meanderings of the mind. Yet this particular dream stood out and bothered me. A huge flood was overcoming me, its waves menacing and fierce, my resting place submerged. Somehow it prepared me for some devastating news and a difficult test. Without a doubt, those first few years were hard, but I came to terms with it all the same.

From where does one find the strength when he learns that perhaps things are not as clear cut as he was told? In England we were advised that the only way to have our own children was through donor insemination—a course of action we would never take—but in Turkey where that is not practiced at all, research has advanced apace to help people in our situation have children of their own. Over there a good number of men with exactly my condition are now fathers, some to twins and triplets. Thus the strain returned as we embarked on a new course of treatment; there was now a possibility that we could have a child, but also the possibility that we would again be disappointed. The treatment running beyond our agreed leave, the strain grew again, the two of us fearing what would happen to our jobs. The financial and emotional burden grew and we wondered from where our strength would come.

There had been so many times that I had read the phrase, 'There is no strength except with Allah,' but sometimes we have to put advice into practice before we see the truth of something. To rely solely on your Creator is one of the most beautiful aspects of faith. Sleepless for four nights, wandering silently through the streets of Istanbul, anxious about all of this,

I did not know from where I would find my strength. Like so many times before, I lamented that I was not strong enough for this, but instead, finding myself in beautiful mosques, I prayed. Suddenly the situation altered, relief had come. Our employers were sympathetic, our financial situation okay, the high emotions lessened. It was true: there is no strength except with God, the Creator of us all. His signs reveal themselves throughout the passage of our lives, but too often we do not see them.

Everything that we do depends on God. Although the various Christian denominations disagree about the nature of divine decree—and it is largely Roman Catholics who use the phrase, 'God willing'—all true believers recognise their dependence on the One who created them. The Muslim who litters his spoken plans with the phrase, *Insha'Allah*—if God wills—is not alone:

> Now a word with all who say, 'Today or the next day we will go off to such and such a town and spend a year there trading and making money.' Yet you have no idea what tomorrow will bring. What is your life after all? You are no more than a mist, seen for a little while and then disappearing. What you ought to say is: 'If it be the Lord's will, we shall live to do so and so.'[8]

This passage from the *Letter of James* reminds us that we are not self-sufficient; whether we live or die is purely the will of God ﷻ. The words 'God willing' are not code for a lazy 'whatever', but signify our reliance and trust in Him. Whilst some might place their life in God's care only for a moment when faced with disaster, we recognise that it is infinitely better for us if we ask for His help in all of our affairs. 'Call upon Me,' says God, 'I will answer you.'

Muslim and Christian theology does not always sit side by side so comfortably, however. Christian authors often allege that the Qur'an misunderstands the Trinity: Christians do not worship three gods as Muslims claim, they argue, but one God made up of three co-equal parts. Meanwhile the Muslim counters that this argument is itself based on a misunderstanding of Islam's teaching on the unity of God. Islam teaches that the only thing that is worthy of worship is the Creator and Sustainer of all things. Anything that is worshipped beside God is described as 'a god'. It does not make any difference whether it is an idol, a tree, a river or a person; if an individual takes it as an object of worship, it is then for that person a god. The Christian retort, of course, is that Jesus ﷺ is God. They recognise that God is One and that to worship other than God is unacceptable: 'You shall have no other gods before Me.'[9] This, the Christian argues, is what the Muslim fails to understand; Jesus ﷺ is not a separate god, but God Himself.

Yet this remains a misunderstanding of the Islamic perspective. There are three world religions that acknowledge the life of Jesus ﷺ: Christianity, Judaism and Islam. While Judaism implicitly denies that he was the Messiah, Muslims acknowledge Jesus ﷺ as a messenger of God, believe in his miracles and consider his mother the best woman of all creation. Islam does emphasise, however, that Jesus ﷺ was not God, insisting instead that he was a prophet sent to the House of Israel. Thus it does not make any difference if a person brings philosophical arguments to say that he was God; the Qur'an's position stays the same. In teaching that Jesus ﷺ is other than God, the fact that Christians worship him means that he is a god worshipped alongside the Creator. Let us suppose that the leader of the opposition, despairing at the party's election prospects, suddenly started claiming that he is God. Naturally we would all agree that he is not and so, even if he told us that he was one in essence with Him, we still would not accept it. The mere presence of an argument does not prove anything.

Still, theologians will no doubt continue to argue this point for years to come, for in the case of both traditions it is the crux of faith. The belief in the Trinity as expressed in the *Nicene Creed* was not arrived at overnight, but came about after a great deal of debate and disagreement. Everyone has heard of Arius who believed that the Father, Son and Holy Spirit were entirely different, sharing neither nature nor essence, but there were hundreds of others who held different viewpoints. Having gone to such lengths to establish what constitutes orthodoxy in the Christian tradition, a meeting of minds between Christian and Muslim obviously remains unlikely. Even so, both traditions agree that our Lord is forgiving and merciful.

Forgiveness

Were we unable to sin, I often wonder, would we appreciate God's mercy? Of course His mercy surrounds us: our hearts which beat without us giving thought, the rain which falls from the sky giving life to dead earth, the air which expands our breasts. But I wonder: were it not for our ability to sin and err, and return to Him in repentance, would we truly understand the blessings He bestows on us?

Nicky Gumbel—of Alpha Course fame—claimed in his book, *Searching Issues*, that in Islam sinners will face judgement without forgiveness, but nothing could be further from the truth. Every chapter of the Qur'an but one begins, 'In the name of God, the Most Gracious, the Most Merciful,' while forgiveness itself is returned to repeatedly throughout its pages. In his chapter entitled *What About Other Religions*, however, Gumbel wrote:

> Secondly, Jesus is unique in his achievement. As Peter asserts, 'salvation is found in no-one else, for there is no other name under heaven given to men, by which we must be saved' (Acts 4:12). We all need a saviour because we have all sinned and we cannot save ourselves from the results of sin. None of the other great religions even claims to have a saviour. ... Muhammad is regarded as a prophet—not as a saviour. In Islam, sinners will face judgement without forgiveness.

> By contrast, Jesus is the one who brings salvation. He
> saves us from our guilt, he saves us from the addictive
> power of sin and he saves us from the judgement we all
> deserve.[10]

It is as if the author cannot conceive of stepping beyond the
bounds of his own theological framework in considering other
faiths. Only in the context of his earlier assertion—that we all
need a saviour—is his statement about Islam true, for it is
indeed the case that a Muslim believes that no name under
heaven has the ability to forgive our sins against God. This does
not mean, however, that there can be no forgiveness. What
Gumbel's position suggests is that God alone is unable to accept
the repentance of one who turns to Him.

One year I spent Easter weekend staying in a rural rectory in
the north of England, my hosts busy with services for the
duration of my stay: the station of the cross on Good Friday
after the night vigil on Thursday and evening worship on
Saturday. At dawn on Sunday my hosts led their congregations
in another vigil, following it with the main service later in the
morning. It was Easter weekend, marking the key events upon
which their entire theology hangs: the crucifixion, the burial
and the resurrection.

Christians believe that the crucifixion represents the ultimate
example of God's love, the only means by which we are
forgiven for our sins. Thus that weekend was a time of emotion
for them, a time for reflection and giving thanks. It was a
period of contemplation, and so I found myself reflecting on
their theology too. The walls of my hosts' study were lined with
books, mostly on different aspects of Christology. They have
pondered their faith deeply for years, and they believe in it with
passion, considering it an altogether coherent philosophy. They
live and breathe this theology. It is everything to them.

My reflections, however, carried me elsewhere. To my mind,
the ultimate example of God's compassion is not found in a
ransom. Instead it is found in that beautiful and humbling

moment when we turn to Him alone, regardless of what we have done, repenting sincerely. He does not require a sacrifice or an atoning saviour. He merely asks us to turn to Him in repentance and He will forgive us. As my hosts dwelt on the cross and the empty tomb that weekend, my thoughts were set on the words of the Qur'an, on the supplications we are taught to say when we err and on a famous *Hadith Qudsi*:

> O son of Adam, so long as you call upon Me and ask of Me, I shall forgive you for what you have done, and I shall not mind. O son of Adam, were your sins to reach the clouds of the sky and were you then to ask forgiveness of Me, I would forgive you. O son of Adam, were you to come to Me with sins nearly as great as the earth and were you then to face Me, ascribing no partner to Me, I would bring you forgiveness nearly as great as it.[11]

To me, that indicates an infinitely more generous Lord: my sins could be like mountains, but God promises forgiveness so long as I turn to Him. No cross, no tomb, no crown of thorns: just simple words from a sincere heart.

Contrary to Gumbel's belief, forgiveness in fact lies at the heart of the Muslim worldview, with frequent references made to repentance throughout the Qur'an, *hadith* and works of Muslim scholars. His view that 'sinners will face judgement without forgiveness' is quite wrong, unless he is speaking of those who do not repent or who reject the message, in which case the position of Christianity is the same. In Islam, the term is 'turning back'—*tawbah*—meaning to turn back to God, seeking refuge in His forgiveness, so that He might turn back to the person who has sinned. Indeed, our Prophet ﷺ taught the following supplication to his followers:

> O God, You are my Lord—there is no god but You. You created me, and I am Your servant; and I uphold Your covenant and promise to You as much as I am able. I seek

refuge in You from the evil I have done. I acknowledge my sin, so forgive me. Indeed, there is none who can forgive sins except You.

In Islam there is no concept of original sin: although the Qur'an tells the story of Adam and Eve, we read that after Adam عليه السلام sinned, he returned in repentance and God forgave him: 'Lo! He is the relenting, the Merciful.'[12] It was not necessary for a redeemer to come to save us from the results of sin thousands of years after the fall of Sumer, for all of us are accountable for only our own deeds and intentions. Islam has a positive view of mankind, recognising that while we have the potential to sink to the depths of depravity, the ability to soar great heights is also within our grasp. The Qur'an states:

Say: Shall I seek another than God for Lord, when He is Lord of all things? Each soul earns only on its own account, nor does any laden bear another's load. Then unto your Lord is your return and He will tell you that wherein you differed.[13]

It is the Muslim's belief that we are each personally responsible for the ultimate destination of our soul and that we have the capacity to rise above our basest desires—if we make the effort. It is not for another to save us from guilt or from the addictive power of sin, as the parable of the prodigal son in the *Gospel of Luke* makes clear. In Islam, reform takes the place of guilt.

Judgement

During my days without faith, when caught in the grip of sin, I used to say, 'God curse me, let me burn in hell.' As an agnostic living in the slipstream of a contemporary reinterpretation of heaven and hell such a remark was so easily said. It was as if to say two things: I cannot help my sinfulness and hell could not be all that bad really. Indeed, many Christians today no longer think of hell in the traditional terms of centuries past. There is ample evidence of this in Christian literature: we find that hell is often described merely as a feeling of alienation from God. As a result, the whole notion of judgement appears somewhat sketchy: 'I could never myself believe in God, if it were not for the Cross,' said a prominent Anglican evangelist some years back. Only a God who had suffered as mankind suffers, the argument goes, could have any right to judge them.

For Muslims, belief in the Day of Judgement, Paradise and Hell is indisputable. Each of these elements is very real. In the Islamic worldview, the life we are living now is preparation for the great examination of the Day of Judgement. It is only necessary to consider the suffering which many have endured to see that Muslims do not share the unorthodox reservations of some Christians. One of the first individuals to embrace Islam during the lifetime of Muhammad ﷺ was an Abyssinian slave named Bilal. In order to demonstrate his opposition to Islam the chief of one of the Meccan clans would take him into the desert each day where he would beat him severely and torture him, repeatedly demanding that he renounce Islam and declare that he believed in the handcrafted idols. Bilal, however, would only repeat that God is One. Later in the early years of Islam, the Meccan tribes placed a boycott on the Muslims, forcing them into starvation. The Muslims, however, continued to affirm that God is One, believing that they would face the Day of Recompense. In fact, Muslims believe that striving through affliction can be a means of expiating sins.

Today I would not dream of uttering those words which once so easily slipped from my tongue. When despairing at my sinful soul, today I can only plead, 'O my Lord, forgive me, turn me from my sins and save me from the Fire.' The Day of Judgement is something to truly fear, for every deed we put forth in this life, good or bad, will be recalled.

Protestants—brought up on the apostle Paul's appeal to Grace and his sustained condemnation of legalism in his letter to the

Galatians—are sometimes heard lamenting the Muslim's insistence on living by the letter of the Law. Grace sets mankind free from all that, they will argue, but surely the state of the world around us bears witness to the fallacy of that view. Some people are indeed blessed with great self-restraint, but some of us might argue that Islam is simply realistic about the strength of individuals and communities.

Yes, some people are just good folk, and yes, some people can become good folk with the promise of reward. But it is true too that some of us must be deterred from deeds which are harmful to us and others. In truth it is few that live by Grace; like donkeys, most of us will only respond to a carrot or a stick, or both depending on our state of mind. I appreciate possessing a faith which is realistic about human nature. I appreciate possessing a faith that does not simply tell me that mankind is born in sin and can do nothing about it except rejoice that a ransom has been paid on my behalf. I appreciate possessing a framework through which I might overcome that which holds me back.

I sometimes feel quite sad that I do not have the pure, beautiful, sound heart of some of my fortunate brothers and sisters in faith. Sometimes we meet people whose whole being exudes kindness. I envy such people a lot, but I also recognise that all is not lost for me. The *sunna*, the Law, this noble framework for our lives, is a blessing for those of us who need a little more help. In our lives, we sometimes deprive ourselves of certain pleasures, for which we are often derided by those around us, but we do so because we know that, in the long run, it is good for us. At other times, we expend our efforts on tasks which we may find a burden, which we may even dislike, but we persevere nevertheless because we know that it is good for us, our family or our community.

Although Protestants differ on this point, Roman Catholics believe that faith in Jesus ﷺ must be accompanied by works. Presumably one who believes that faith in Jesus ﷺ alone leads to salvation does not need to think very much about the Hour.

It is, however, very much in the mind of the practising Muslim. When preparing for a journey we always spend some time thinking about what we should take with us: this is the likeness of the Muslim preparing for the Day of Judgement. He or she is not thinking much about this life, for it is only a temporary realm. 'Be in this world as a stranger or a traveller,' the Prophet ﷺ told one of his companions.[14] God granted mankind this life in order that we might prepare for our return to Him.

It was in despair at my propensity to slip that I used to utter some hideous words, but I was not alone. Others philosophise about the hereafter: some demand a suffering judge, some want a hell wherein man experiences only alienation from God. A Christian colleague at work, arguing with a passionate atheist who insisted on deriding the beliefs of religious folk as the legends of peoples past, recently defended her belief in Heaven courageously; but, she said, she was not sure that she believed in Hell. Nowadays, some people afford themselves the luxury of believing whatever they like so long as it is not a 'salvation issue'. Muslims, however, believe that there is a reality, one which is defined by God. They believe in the Day of Judgement, in Paradise and Hell, and the sincere act with this is mind.

As our lives hurtle along apace, we wonder what will become of us tomorrow and what can be said of our store of good deeds. As Muslims we are taught that when we are gathered back together on that Revered Day we shall protest that we lived our life for but a day. It will be as if time had not dragged on at all. Pondering the swift passage of time, a dear friend proposed that we should understand the saying of our Blessed Prophet ﷺ that time will decrease as the Hour approaches as meaning that the value of time will decrease. Our days, he noted, have been chopped into the smallest of units and the more an item of value is chopped into smaller articles, its value reduces correspondingly. Thus we are troubled by a minute's delay, whilst our predecessors were happy to journey for a day, noting that the angels travel down to earth in a day the like of which is 1,000 years. I believe there is truth in his view, but none of it weakens the approach of the Hour. As I look back on the speed with which the past five years have passed me by there is a sense of regret. Time is all we have; as said another friend, time is the most breathtaking of our Lord's creation. It is both unfathomable and true; He can stop it at will and extend it without limit. Indeed, He promises that our days in this fleeting abode will seem like nought compared to the days of the hereafter.

As another week passes us by it is only natural that we ask what we have done to draw closer to our Lord. Conversely, what has distracted us and led us away? Are we on call to every whim of the breaking news? Are we reactionaries, darting in one direction and then another, led by every plot and plan? Believing that we are doing good, we jeopardise our obligations in our race to respond to every provocation placed before us.

We have no idea what will become of us tomorrow as time hurtles along; taking stock of our store of deeds, we recognise that time is too precious. When we are gathered back together on the Day of Judgement, we will complain that we tarried for just a few hours, but our complaints will have no impact. On that Day, all truth will be known.

Some months ago, a national newspaper carried a story about the tendency that exists amongst the ordinary man to believe in conspiracy theories. From the assassination of political leaders to the premature death of a famous person and from technological achievements to acts of war, the official story always seems to be accompanied by numerous counter explanations. There exists in mankind a yearning for truth and yet we recognise that our appreciation of reality can only ever be partial.

When in the afternoon of 11 September, 2001, our production manager at work informed us that somebody had flown a plane into one of the towers of the World Trade Centre in New York, my initial foreboding thought was that Muslims were involved. I was not aware of the scale at that stage: in my mind, I had the picture of a single-prop Cessna and the memory of the 1993 plot to explode a bomb underneath the towers. When I returned home that evening and saw the images on the television news, that initial reaction changed. Overtaken by emotion, I was physically sick, the recurring images burning onto my retinas, and I could no longer accept that initial conclusion of mine. This was not the action of a single mad man, incinerating himself as his plane disintegrated as it crashed through the windows; here was a calculated, co-ordinated act of extreme brutality in which two commercial jets had been flown with absolute precision to their destination, massacring a civilian population. As one who had studied the concept of war in Islamic Law, which prohibits any action that would cause harm to non-combatants—even to the extent that Muslim soldiers may not chop the enemy's fruit trees down—I could not accept that Muslims were responsible.

Thus when an ordinarily sensible friend sent me a link to an article on the internet that disputed the official story, I—like many otherwise intelligent individuals—found myself clinging to alternative theories and the many questions that remained unanswered. It did not help that the media had been reporting dubious tales about the terrorist mastermind's passport being found in the rubble of the World Trade Centre, not to mention a 'Smoking Gun' video that featured a fat Osama Bin Laden— nor that the anthrax spores released over the subsequent days were eventually traced back to government facilities.

For several months I would be found scouring the internet for 'the truth', looking for evidence that 'we'd been set up'. Much of the speculation was clearly detritus originating with right-wing Christians, Millenniumists, Messianists, Supremacists and others united on pro-gun, anti-federal government, anti-UN and anti-Semitic politics, often with strong views about a move towards a one-world-government and a new-world-order: whackos in common parlance. Still, the doubts remained and all of us wanted to prove that Muslims had no part in that horrific act. In time, I came across the declassified document concerning Operation Northwoods which had been published on the National Security Archive's website in 1998. This 1962 proposal presented various outline plans of action that could be used to garner public and international support for US military intervention in Cuba. The suggestions included staging sabotages and sinking an American ship at the US military base at Guantanamo Bay and blaming it on Cuban forces, hijacking civilian planes, sinking boats carrying refugees fleeing Cuba and setting up terrorist attacks in Washington and Miami, and blaming them on the Communists.

Unlike the wild speculation of the internet's gathering of eccentrics, most of whom had their own quite unpleasant agendas, here was a genuine declassified document which could be viewed independently of the united anti-something extremists. However unlikely it was that the actions of 2001 were part of some grand conspiracy on the part of employees of the state, this document was evidence that a precedent of past intent existed. Somewhat naively, I wrote to Jon Snow at Channel 4 News, pointing him towards the National Security Archive located at The George Washington University. He wrote back to tell me that he would look into it. A week later he went off to New York to see the devastating carnage first-hand where he would have concluded—as I did later—that Northwoods was just a long-forgotten historical document. Soon afterwards Channel 4 broadcast a documentary debunking some of the conspiracy theories associated with that fateful day.

Over the years since then I have received my fair share of emails exploring one alleged conspiracy or other. Obsessed with *isnad,* however, I am the kind of person who feels compelled to trace emails back to their source—claims about computer viruses that not even the best brains of Symantec, Norton and Microsoft put together can fix have taken their toll on me—and so most of my friends have learnt to leave this cynical character off their mailing lists. Occasionally I revert to thinking that things may not be as they seem, but I am generally no longer interested for we believe in the Day of Judgement when all truth will be told.

When a massacre occurred in London in July 2005, I managed to avoid the conspiracy theories for a whole week. Most of the Muslims I know had long been saying that it was only a matter of time before one of the extremists in our midst did something like this. Indeed, after the Madrid train bombings I found myself looking at my fellow passengers suspiciously on my way to and from work.

When the explosions occurred that day, I desperately hoped that it was the action of extreme anarchists timed to coincide with the G8 Summit, but I somehow knew that this was unlikely. Working in the National Health Service, our organisation had been put on standby for an evacuation of injured people as London hospitals filled up. The initial estimates of number of dead were in the high hundreds, far out-numbering the eventual death toll, and all normal work ceased as we went into emergency-response mode.

For the days that followed, my anger was intense. Selfishly, my initial thoughts were around how I would have felt had it been my wife who had been cut to pieces, for until a month earlier that shattered Edgware Road train took us to work every day. Selfishly too, my thoughts were about this spelling the end to Muslim life in Britain, for at work uncomfortable comments were being made about Muslims all around me.

A few days later, however, a link to the BBC's audio archive arrived in my inbox and I found myself listening to the famous interview in which crisis management expert, Peter Powers, explained that he had been running a walk-through of a simulated terrorist act which was premised on bombs going off simultaneously at the same stations that had been targeted in the actual attack, at exactly the same time that morning. It was not long before I was listening to the archive on the BBC website, catching his comments on Radio Five Live. Although we later learned that the walk-through was simply a paper-based exercise of little significance, I was soon saying to my friends, 'things may not be as they seem', but they probably were. Thank goodness we believe in the Day of Judgement.

Perhaps conspiracy theories are convenient for us, helping us to avoid taking ourselves to account. Seeing a plot where there is none—almost to the point wherein the plotters are considered omnipotent—is considered preferable to putting our house in order.

To be fair, there are some quite valid reasons why many of us chase after alleged conspiracies from time to time and it is not always tired anti-Americanism and anti-Semitism as is often alleged. Quite apart from the fact that Islam prohibits in-discriminate violence and forbids suicide, it is sadly true that we are all too familiar with the current state of the Muslim community. Al-Qaeda is seen as a ruthlessly efficient operation, but we know the state of our mosques, the disrepair of which provides clear evidence of a lack of organisational skills on the part of their members. A key characteristic of Al-Qaeda operations is said to be the use of synchronised bombing and yet we live in a community famed for its laxity around punc-tuality: it is so bad that lateness is the first non-*sunna* a convert picks up upon becoming Muslim. Sleeper cells are apparently able to launch operations on their own and yet we have difficulties taking the initiative to clean the dishes left in the corner from *iftar* a year ago. Of course, I am being cynical—perhaps in ignorance—but these are genuinely the kinds of thoughts that cross our minds every time we hear of complex Muslim plots.

There have been occasions when I would have been happy to believe in some of the conspiracy theories knocking around on the internet and in the cafes of Westminster's Edgware Road. The one-world-government new-world-order theory that makes much of George H W Bush's speech on 11 September, 1990, has its appeal: why get out of bed in the morning when we know that everything is being controlled by an all-powerful group of individuals? Unfortunately, despite its origin in funda-mentalist Christian eschatology, today's Muslims are investing in this nationalist ideology to their detriment. With each act of barbarity that seems to be the work of Muslims, some sort of need to explain it away arises. Seeking out conspiracy theories is the easy response, but real Muslims are people of truth. If we do not know where the truth lies, we rely on our Creator with whom stands all truth. On that awesome Day which will last 50,000 years, all truth will be made apparent. There is wisdom in our Creator's great plan.

Today we can travel between different locations faster than ever before, whizzing along in our cars. Journeys that once took weeks, months, even years, can now be covered in hours. When I arose this morning I did not have to go out of my house to draw water for the day. In mid-winter I do not need to venture outdoors for fuel. At night there is no running around getting lamps lit. I arrive at work just after eight and leave again just after four. I have more time on my hands than the generations of the previous millennium and yet I complain that I do not have enough time to do everything that needs to be done.

And so what will be my excuse before my Lord on that awesome Day when I will complain that I tarried on the Earth for but a matter of hours, for that will be as it seemed on a day lasting 50,000 years? That the internet evaporated my evenings? That I was too busy to seek knowledge? My life is ease and I have no excuse. For followers of the two traditions, it is a reality that is drawing near.

Histories

Muslims and Christians hold much in common by way of their beliefs and yet so often it is as if a great chasm divides us. The Muslims in the news seem so alien and yet that lovely Muslim doctor at the hospital seems so friendly and sincere. Nowadays there is much talk of identity, of what it means to belong and of shared values, but sometimes there seems to be an assumption that we must all trace our values back to Hellenic roots as if this were the sole foundation of civilisation. My heart, however, has always felt comfort in the Semitic pathway. As a child, the Parables spoke to me, but Paul's epistles did not. As an agnostic it was the *Letter of James*.

My burgundy-bound Bible from those days before faith is filled with scribbles in pencil, with scruffy underlining and highlighter ink: the etchings of a searching soul—but one book stands out. On the title page of the *Letter of James* there is a handwritten note which reads, 'The most beautiful book in the Bible.' I was yet to learn of Islam—yet to tread this path—but looking back now it seems clear to me that the author was a Muslim of the era before Muhammad ﷺ. I am not alone in reaching this conclusion. James' address of the 12 tribes dispersed throughout the land nods to the Judaic-Christian world, whose resemblance to another tradition has been widely noted over the years: 'the traditional and historical parallels between early Judaic-Christianity and Islam are inescapable.'[15] Indeed, while I would naturally dispute the case of dependence given my belief in revelation, Hans-Joachim Schoeps wrote in *Theology and History of Jewish Christianity*:

> Though it may not be possible to establish exact proof of the connection, the indirect dependence of Mohammed on sectarian Jewish Christianity is beyond any reasonable doubt. This leaves us with a paradox of truly world-historical dimensions: the fact that while Jewish Christianity in the Church came to grief, it was preserved in Islam and, with regard to some of its driving impulses at least, it has lasted till our own time.[16]

When I put the teachings of the *Letter of James* and the teachings of Islam side by side, the similarities are striking. Several years ago I began work on a small text that would do just that, for I felt that the parallel presentation conveyed meanings that have sadly escaped many. Much is made of difference when we encounter the other, but there is a great deal to be gained from highlighting the common ground.

The reality of the focus on identity, on what it means to belong, on shared values, is that what defines our present is a hugely diverse past. While the phrase 'our Judeo-Christian heritage' has emerged over recent years, that old focus on Hellenic and Grecian ancestry remains dominant. The truth, however, is that Semitic pathways have had a huge influence on our culture. Indeed, there is ample evidence that Europe would not have advanced as it has in science and philosophy had Semitic peoples not translated those ancient works held in such esteem: we are indebted more to Andalusia, note some of the more generous historians of our age, than to ancient Greece and Rome.

It might be said that the best starting point for any dialogue between faiths is at the beginning, returning to the fundamentals of a religion and therefore to its earliest history. A definition of fundamentalism that implies a study of history should be viewed in a positive light, recognising the origins and primal teachings of our beliefs. On Christmas Eve 2002 I listened as an Anglican bishop explained that the historical figure of Jesus ﷽ was not of key importance to believers of his faith; what mattered, he argued, was what Jesus ﷽ means to Christians today. This view is in fact illogical for if, as Muslims contend, Jesus ﷽ was actually a prophet calling his people to the worship of one God, to then worship him as God would be to go against his teaching. Similarly, if, as Christians hold, he may be taken as an object of worship, then to deny his divinity would also be of consequence. In other words, the historical person of Jesus ﷽—and Muhammad ﷺ—is of great importance. It is peculiar then that the view that the figure of Jesus ﷽ in faith is more important than the historic person is held by a fair number of contemporary Christian theologians, recognising that the gospels present the kerygma, not an accurate historical record.

At one extreme, the writings of John Hick in *The Metaphor of God Incarnate* seem to make a mockery of the notion that there is religious truth. If faith becomes merely what we make

it, how does that help us? If Jesus ﷺ himself did not teach that
he was God incarnate dying for the sins of the world, as Hick
argued, is the idea that divine incarnation should be understood
merely as a metaphor not simply another way of saying, 'It
doesn't matter what he taught; I wish to believe this'?

While many theologians reject Hick's thesis, their writings
nevertheless follow a similar pattern. Against this backdrop, a
definition of fundamentalism as being the conviction that the
authentic version of a faith is most likely to be found in its
earliest period makes perfect sense. To follow our teachers, be it
Jesus ﷺ in the case of Christianity or Muhammad ﷺ in the
case of Islam, it is obvious that we should know what they
themselves taught.

Unfortunately this task is not necessarily easy. Christian
fundamentalism is often frowned upon precisely because the
paucity of source material makes constructing a picture of
historical reality difficult. Traditionally the image of Jesus ﷺ
has been based almost wholly on the narrations contained
within the four Gospels, with two references to his life in the
writings of Josephus now considered later Christian inter-
polations. Today the apocryphal writings of the Church, and
the Dead Sea Scrolls and Nag Hamadi Library are viewed by
some as a secondary source.[17]

The contemporary belief that each gospel was written to
present a different face of Christ highlights the problem we
encounter. If the primary sources themselves were written with
the intention of converting non-Christians and strengthening
the faith of believers, the biographer of Jesus' ﷺ life must face
the possibility that material considered unimportant in conveying
a particular message has been omitted by the original authors.
It is well known that if we collect all the words actually spoken
by Jesus ﷺ in the four Gospels, removing duplicate passages,
they fit on no more than two sides of a sheet of A4 paper. Given
the impact Jesus ﷺ is said to have had on the life of countless
generations of Christians, this is a woefully small amount of
information.

The gospels do not tell us what language Jesus ﷺ spoke, with Aramaic, Hebrew, Greek, Syriac and a Galilaean dialect of Chaldic all having been suggested as possibilities by scholars of Christianity. The gospels fail to teach us any of the doctrines later adopted by the church, although we note that the *Nicene Creed* is 41 lines longer than the earliest creed known to us.[18] Nor do the gospels help us to understand that Palestine at the time was under Roman occupation; they are lacking in both historical and geographical accuracy. More importantly, the gospels do not tell us anything about the authors of the books; we are merely provided with first names and are then left to guess their relationship to Jesus ﷺ, whether they were eye-witnesses to the events of his life, whether they were known for their honesty and what their role in the early church was. The seasoned argument that the four gospels prove to be reliable witnesses by virtue of the fact that they agree on the main points but differ on a few of the details, pointing to the fact that the authors did not collude in their accounts, is unsurprisingly not supported by many biblical scholars. Evidence of copying from Mark is brought out by some, whilst others argue for the existence of an earlier primal document which they label Q.

It is perhaps predictable, therefore, that many Christians are cynical about fundamentalism and its claim to seek the authentic version of a faith in the earliest period. Yet this concern is not necessarily universal. By contrast, the earliest Muslims took the preservation of the Islamic message extremely seriously, providing us with a rich source of information about Muhammad's ﷺ appearance, conduct, manners and tastes. We know what he looked like, the colour of his hair, how he dressed and the speed of his walk, which is why the infamous controversy about cartoons said to depict the Prophet ﷺ passed many practising Muslims by: the illustrations bore no resemblance to him whatsoever, but reminded us of early 20th-century caricatures of the great scheming hook-nosed Jew instead.

In terms of substance, the collected sayings and deeds of Muhammad ﷺ—known as the *hadith*—would be equated with the gospels, since the Qur'an is considered a book of revelation brought down by the Angel Gabriel. It is notable that the Muslim community was concerned with documenting and committing to memory every verse of the Qur'an during the lifetime of Muhammad ﷺ himself. In their midst, he dictated, explained and arranged every verse of the Qur'an and, following his death, his community took it upon itself to continue to preserve it meticulously. It was precisely because the Qur'an states that the previous scriptures had been corrupted from within that the Muslim community considered it crucial to put in place mechanisms that would preserve the final revelation.

When I set out to learn the Qur'an myself I was struck by the absolute precision demanded by my teacher, each pronunciation analysed in great depth, each verse studied as I tried to commit it to memory. In turn, the same is required of him by his teacher as he moves from memorising the entire Qur'an to mastering each of the dialects in which it was revealed. Indeed, the same is true of his teacher's teacher as the science passes from generation to generation.

In order to safeguard both the Qur'an and the narrations concerning the details of Muhammad's ﷺ life his community established an elaborate structure based on the law of witness to diminish the risks usually encountered when passing information on from one person to another.[19] During his lifetime his companions would relate his words and actions to one another by saying, 'The Prophet said/did such and such.' When such a report was mentioned to a further person the source would be related along with what was said or done: 'Aisha said the Prophet ﷺ said such and such.'[20]

As time passed by, the scholars of Islam insisted on carefully examining the source of all information which they received so that by the end of the first century of the Muslim calendar the practice had become a science in its own right. For a report to be accepted, scholars demanded that four conditions be met: that it was accurate, that all narrators in the chain of narration were trustworthy, that the chain of transmission was unbroken and that there was positive support for the statement from all other available evidence.

During the second half of the first century of the Muslim calendar, the sayings of Muhammad ﷺ began to be categorised by subject in booklets. Again the scholars considered it necessary to establish a means of protecting the content of these books from possible adulteration. They therefore required any scholar involved in passing on his sayings to be in direct contact with the person to whom they were being passed. So insistent were they on the role of witness that they considered the use of a book without hearing it from the author tantamount to giving false evidence. One could not contemplate adaptations such as the incorporation of material from the Dead Sea Scrolls into the gospels at the beginning of the 21st century, or the 9th-century addition of the story of the adulteress in John's gospel. A personal commentary added to a book had to be signed, or else it would be considered to invalidate the text. Rigorous controls were instated even when it came to using books of the sayings of Muhammad ﷺ where reading certificates which amounted to licences were mandatory. When transmitting such books, a detailed record of the attendance at the gathering was taken and added to the reading certificate, which then became an exclusive authorisation for those listed in it to read, teach, copy or quote from that book. Other checks were also employed to ensure that sacred knowledge was preserved in a suitably respectful manner.

Early in my journey of faith I became interested in the issue of safeguarding knowledge now that technology had brought publishing within virtually anyone's grasp. As a new Muslim I was interested in the question of what constituted knowledge, given that I was able to lay my hands on any number of books on Islamic topics without really knowing anything about their authors. It was because of this that I decided to write my post-graduate dissertation on this subject, proposing a concept of review and accreditation for popular Islamic publishing in the United Kingdom.

More recently I began reflecting on this once more after encountering several instances of individuals sharing sincere advice with others on matters pertaining to our religion. The act in itself may have been commendable, but I was troubled by the fact that the advice was offered by those who cared not to reveal their name. One would understand that someone in fear of their life or prosecution might seek refuge in anonymity, but each of the cases I witnessed had been quite straightforward: the photographer receiving an anonymous letter warning him about his trade; the commentary on music published by a concerned anonymous Muslim; a writer given firm but kind advice by one who did not reveal their name.

Compare this to the enlightened days of our community. A reading certificate defined which books scholars could use, while a record of regular attendance was always kept by those promulgating books of *hadith*. Details were kept of who had listened to the entire book, who had joined in partially, which portions they had missed and the dates and location of the readings. The certificate was an exclusive licence for those listed within to read, teach, copy and quote from that book.[21]

Muslims were so concerned about the preservation of their teachings that an entire science developed to determine the authenticity of *hadith*. In their *Guide to Sira and Hadith Literature in Western Languages* Anees and Athar wrote about the science of *hadith*: 'It is the only branch of knowledge that requires personal ethical responsibility on the part of individuals who involve themselves in this endeavour. In its quest for exactitude, it held accountable those who transmitted information.'[22]

By contrast, in the case of my recent encounters we did not know if the anonymous author was X, son of Y, student of Z, nor where they had obtained their learning. Consequently I found myself pondering the question I had first asked when I was very new to Islam. At the time—considering an Islamic heritage that placed great emphasis on the authentication of knowledge—I was interested in whether there was a case for the establishment of a review body, modelled not just on

Muslim tradition but also on the structures of peer review set up in the scientific and academic publishing industries.

In a society that argues that there is no absolute truth, only contingent truths, the claim that Islamic knowledge needs protection can obviously be considered an affront to the concept of freedom of speech—indeed, to the freedom of individual Muslims to make their own *fatwa*. Two authors writing about publishing in Muslim countries almost a decade ago noted that the books now published by Muslims in great quantities, 'set aside the long tradition of authoritative discourse by religious scholars in favour of a direct understanding of texts. Today chemists and medical doctors can interpret Islamic principles as equals with scholars who have graduated from traditional centres of learning.'[23]

While many advocates of unrestricted free speech would welcome such a development, I argued that apart from opening our religion to the general threat of corruption, it could be used to support actions which have disastrous consequences. I had in mind wanton acts of violence, but the possibilities are endless. I was in favour, therefore, of the tradition which saw Islamic scholars confident of their role as guardians of knowledge. I noted that, writing in *Knowledge Triumphant: The Concept of Knowledge in Medieval Islam*, Franz Rosenthal argued that there was little that later influences and developments were able to accomplish by way of injecting new ideas into what constituted Islamic knowledge.[24]

I was once asked how I could accept one book of the Bible while rejecting all the others when I sought to draw attention to the teachings of the *Letter of James* after I had become a Muslim. The question threw me because there was no sense that I accepted it over or in place of others; it merely interested me. All of us read books at times with which we disagree or which conflict with our own beliefs; because they sit on our bookshelves it does not mean that we concur with the words contained therein. In the case of religious texts, my view is coloured by the sciences established by the believers of my faith in centuries past. In this worldview, a text is not considered accurate purely on the basis of emotional attachment—like mine for the *Letter of James*—but rather as a result of exacting scholarship.

In Muslim tradition, a report concerned with matters of religion was always scrutinised for reliability on the basis of two factors: the study of the text itself and consideration of its chain of narration. The well-known orientalist, Montgomery Watt, explained:

> The chains of transmitters were therefore carefully scrutinised to make sure that the persons named could in fact have met one another, that they could be trusted to repeat the story accurately, and that they did not hold any heretical views. This implied extensive biographical studies; and many biographical dictionaries have been preserved giving the basic information about a man's teachers and pupils, the views of later scholars and the date of his death.[25]

When a Muslim considers the reports presented in the Bible by contrast, the first thing with which he or she is faced is the absence of a chain of narration. The Jewish scholar, Bernard Lewis, wrote:

> From an early date Muslim scholars recognized the danger of false testimony and hence false doctrine, and developed an elaborate science for criticizing tradition. 'Traditional science', as it was called, differed in many respects from modern historical source criticism, and modern scholarship has always disagreed with evaluations of traditional scientists about the authenticity and accuracy of ancient narratives. But their careful scrutiny of the chains of transmission and their meticulous collection and preservation of variants in the transmitted narratives give to medieval Arabic historiography a professionalism

and sophistication without precedent in antiquity and without parallel in the contemporary medieval West. By comparison, the historiography of Latin Christendom seems poor and meagre, and even the more advanced and complex historiography of Greek Christendom still falls short of the historical literature of Islam in volume, variety and analytical depth.[26]

It would be illogical then for me to accept a book of the Bible as authentic when it does not meet the strict criteria required by Muslims in this regard. The biographical information offered at the beginning of this letter, for example, is severely limited. The *Letter of James* has never been a source of my religion, but its address to the believers in Christ amongst the twelve tribes interested me nevertheless, suggesting roots in Christianity's earliest era. In my own studies as an agnostic, one of my major interests was the beliefs and practices of the earliest Christian communities for they should—I hypothesised—have been closest to the religion of Jesus ﷺ. Thus, as a matter of interest I always felt that the *Letter of James* carried great import.

If we claim to follow Jesus ﷺ and Muhammad ﷺ we need to know what they themselves taught which entails going back to the source. During the month of *Rabi' Al-Awwal* each year many Muslims remember our Prophet's ﷺ birth and life. The first time I encountered such commemorations—only a couple of years ago—I listened to a fascinating talk detailing his noble character, followed by recitation of poetry and then dinner.

On another occasion I listened as a group of Muslims, young and old, studied the Prophet's ﷺ *sunna*, reading from an-Nawawi's *Riyad al-Salihin*, before spending over an hour reading poetry about him aloud. As I pondered on those I witnessed expressing such love for the Prophet ﷺ as they read his biography and his *sunna* one year, I realised that I did not know him as I should. Taking note of my distance from his noble example I concluded that I too should pick up his *sira* again and read.

'How can you accept one book of the Bible,' asks an inquisitive voice, 'and reject all the others?' This is a question not just for an eccentric who became obsessed with the 'tiniest spark' in the *Letter of James*, but equally for the various denominations of the Christian church. After all, there is great difference between denominations even now with regard to which books are accepted as canonical and which are not. Historically, the famous case is that of Marcion who sought to reject the whole of the Old Testament, claiming that the loving Father of the New Testament was a different God from that of the Old. Today it could be said that many take a similar stance to Marcion even if they would never actually articulate it, as Walter Moberly wrote:

> For many Christians the Old Testament tends to be more of an embarrassment than a resource, more of a stone to trip over than a well to drink from. The ghost of Marcion, who in the second century was the first Christian seriously to propose that Christians did not need, and would be better off without those Scriptures of Israel which came to be known as the Old Testament, still haunts many a Christian mind. Although the official position of the churches down the centuries has been that Marcion was wrong, the actual practice of many churches suggest a position more along the lines of 'he was probably more right than wrong'.[27]

Where the canon of the New Testament is concerned, the debate about which books are considered authoritative has been ongoing for centuries. In his work on the canon of the New Testament, Bruce Metzger presented a huge number that were accepted and rejected at different times throughout the ages.[28] The gospels of Judas, Mani, Mary, Nicodemus, Peter, Philip and Thomas are clearly missing from the accepted canon of our era, as are the infancy gospels, such as the *Gospel of the Nativity of Mary*, while the known lost gospels number at least 23. A number of books which were once considered part of the Roman Catholic New Testament canon, but which are absent today include several of the writings of the Apostolic Fathers. The *Didache* was considered scripture by Clement of Alexandria and Origen. The 5th-century Greek Codex Alexandrius contained the first Epistle of Clement, which was read in services of worship at Corinth around 170CE.[29]

More recently, Ulrich Zwingli insisted that the book of *Revelation* was not part of the New Testament at the Berne Disputation of 1528. Martin Luther called the *Letter of James* an epistle of straw, and denigrated *Jude, Hebrews* and *Revelation*. Although he printed them in his German Bible he explained in their prefaces his doubts about their authority. Andreas Bodenstein of Karlstadt divided the New Testament into sections of different levels, the lowest of which included *James, 2 Peter, 2* and *3 John, Jude, Hebrews* and *Revelations*. Erasmus doubted that Paul was the author of *Hebrews* and James of the *Letter of James*, and questioned the authorship of *2 Peter, 2* and *3 John*, and *Jude*. The Swedish Gustavus Adolphus Bible of 1618 labelled these books as 'Apocryphal New Testament'.[30]

It would be wrong to assume that the Bibles of today are all united upon one canon. Indeed, the major denominations actually differ as to which books they accept and reject. The Protestant Church has the Hebrew canon as its Old Testament, with some books divided, numbering 39 in total. This denomination rejected a number of books and parts of books which were previously included in the Old Testament in the Greek Septuagint and Latin Vulgate. The Protestant New Testament is made up of 27 books. The Roman Catholic Old Testament includes *Tobit, Judith*, the Greek additions to *Esther*, the *Wisdom of Solomon, Sirach, Baruch*, the *Letter of Jeremiah*, the *Prayer of Azariah* and the *Song of the Three Jews, Susanna, Bel and the Dragon, 1 Maccabees* and *2 Maccabees*. In total the Roman Catholic Bible is made up of 73 books. The Greek Orthodox Church has a Bible which includes all the books accepted by the Roman Catholic Church, with the addition of *1 Esdras*, the

Prayer of Manasseh, Psalm 151 and 3 *Maccabees*. The Slavonic canon adds 2 *Esdras*. Other Eastern churches also include 4 *Maccabees*.

It is easy to ask one eccentric how he can accept a book of the Bible while rejecting all the others—as if that were the case—but clearly more difficult to address that question to fellow believers. For those who believe in divine revelation, authority lies at the heart of our way of life. Faith is not belief in doubt or uncertainty: it is confidence, trust and reliance. It is the belief that God has sent us guidance. 'And verily We have raised in every nation a messenger proclaiming: serve God and shun false gods…'[31]

CHAPTER THREE

To Be An English Muslim

The backstreets, parks and squares of central London have an appeal that is sometimes difficult to explain. I used to wander Bloomsbury, Holborn and the Regent's Park—Coram's Fields, Lincoln's Inn, Tavistock Square, Montague Street, Langham Street, Bow Street, Covent Garden—often lost in a world of my own, pondering on all that surrounded me. Friends often spent those weekend evenings in the loud pubs and clubs of the city, but I found myself a silent witness instead, exploring its every street on foot. Sometimes I would find myself returning home to the accompaniment of a beautiful dawn chorus as the sky lightened and turned orange, the sweet song of blackbirds surprising me given the din that characterised WC1. One bank holiday in early May I returned to those streets with purpose. Through study and prayer I had gradually been coming to believe in the religion of Muhammad ﷺ, the Messenger of God, and now a kind of certainty had settled within. Having spent the whole weekend on my own, contemplating the urge to honour God that now dominated me, I emerged from my flat in the early evening and set out along my favourite streets, continuing my innermost conversations as I sauntered onwards. Although the holiday weekend was drawing to a close, Covent Garden was still lively with crowds of people bustling here and there. It was there that I posed a question to myself: 'Will you leave all of this behind?' Perhaps I did not need to, but just then I felt an incredible need to reform myself and start anew, and so this question was quite symbolic. It was as if I was about to leave one world and enter another. 'Will you be able to leave all of this behind?' was what I really meant. I stood in that market square for quite some time, observing the scene all around me as I pondered upon this question. By nightfall I had the answer.

A sentiment commonly expressed by those without faith is that religion should be a private affair and yet they often seem to deny this slogan by their insistence on making what is private public. My testimony of faith came after a very personal journey over the preceding years, months and weeks, but as soon as I made the decision to state those words I found my whole life thrust into public view for all to scrutinise as they pleased. I had considered my utterance of those two simple sentences—I bear witness that none is worthy of worship except God ﷻ and that Muhammad ﷺ is His Messenger—a personal matter, but within only a few hours this news was in the public domain. I had many friends at the start of that day who by sundown refused to speak to me. The questions I had been asking myself the previous evening had suddenly come into sharp focus for I had not anticipated that the reaction of my acquaintances would be quite like that. 'Will you leave all of this behind?'

The reason my answer was yes in every case was that I desperately wanted to honour God, to leave my atheism and agnosticism behind me, and return to Him. This was why I had returned to studying the Bible and to attending church over the previous year despite the derision of my friends: I knew that I needed God and I was desperately seeking truth. I was never put under pressure to convert—in fact I was often perturbed by the reluctance of both Muslims and Christians to share their faith and convince me of its truth—but found myself driven onwards by an overpowering feeling of alienation from God instead. Thus rather than dwell on the reaction of others I busied myself with learning.

Religious belief is not merely centred on faith. Since coming to believe in Islam I have performed a certain ritual over 11,000 times and have prostrated before my Lord around 90,000 times.

These numbers indicate that there are duties which Muslims are obliged to perform as part of their day-to-day lives. From the moment I made my testimony of faith, I established the routine of formal prayer which is performed five times each day at dawn, midday, mid-afternoon, sunset and nightfall, although it did not all come naturally to me. For some weeks I was reliant on handwritten prompts to guide me through the words, only to discover that I knew them off by heart one day when I had to pray alone in unfamiliar surroundings without my scrappy notes. The purpose of this ritual prayer—known as *salat*—is to remind us of the reality of our life in this world, to give us more opportunities to please our Lord and to wash away the sins which we accumulate during the course of any day.

Salat begins with intention and is followed by a succession of actions—standing whilst reciting verses of the Qur'an, bowing whilst praising God, prostrating and kneeling. The opening chapter of the Qur'an is recited in every single prayer—at least 17 times a day if one offers only the obligatory prayers—and reads:

> Praise be to God, Lord of the worlds, the Compassionate, the Merciful, Sovereign of the Day of Judgement! You alone we worship, and to You alone we turn for help. Guide us to the straight path, the path of those whom You have favoured, not of those who have incurred Your anger, nor of those who have gone astray.[32]

While bowing we utter the words, 'Holy is my Lord, the Magnificent.' While prostrating we say, 'Glory to my Lord, the Most High.' This ritual prayer performed five times a day is our means of maintaining a continuous link with God. It is not, of course, our only bond to Him for individuals can pray at any time and in any manner according to the will of the supplicant.

In due course other duties followed such as fasting, paying *zakat* and pilgrimage. While fasting is a voluntary act throughout the rest of the year, it is obligatory during the month of *Ramadan* for all physically able Muslims. Those who are sick, on a journey, pregnant or nursing are permitted to break the fast although they are required to make up an equal number of days later in the year or else feed a needy person for each day they missed. Fasting is regarded principally as a means of purification. By abstaining from normal pleasures and comforts the fasting person achieves growth in their spiritual life, learning discipline, self-restraint, patience and flexibility. Similarly, *zakat*—the etymology of which is to increase, foster and make pure—is the process of giving a proportion of one's wealth to the poor and needy each year. The pilgrimage to Mecca once in a Muslim's lifetime—the *hajj*—is also obligatory for all who are able.

Not every religious duty is an act of ritual, however. Our Prophet ﷺ was asked, 'To whom should I be dutiful?' He replied: 'Your mother.' When he was asked who next, he repeated the same answer two more times, before finally mentioning the man's father.[33] In Islam, breaking the ties of kinship is considered a major sin, listed alongside murder and polytheism. Islam is a religion of action: having good manners, being charitable, looking after orphans and feeding the poor are all duties that Muslims are strongly encouraged to fulfil. If I learnt anything during my earliest days as a Muslim, it was that our path is considered the Middle Way.

When I embraced Islam in 1998, one of the first pieces of advice which I received from Muslim friends was to learn the names of three people and then stay far away from them. They were three men who have since been made infamous by the media as purveyors of extremism: two have been deported from the country, while the third is serving a prison sentence. Shortly afterwards I received an angry email from my father demanding to know whether I had passed his email address on to a group of zealots. He had received a message purportedly sponsored by a vast array of Muslim organisations which told him to convert to Islam or face the consequences. I most certainly had not passed his address on to anybody and glancing at the other names in the bulk mailing list—other public figures in the church—I surmised that his email address had been harvested along with others from Christian websites. Rather distressed by my father's anger I showed the email to a fellow student who had been involved with Hizb-ut-Tahir in the early 1990s who told me that the author—then the leader of a group known as al-Muhajirun—was an eccentric who had had a habit of making up organisation names to make his little band of followers efforts' appear more credible. None of the organisations listed at the end of the email actually existed.

Over the next few years we heard a lot from the trio I was told to avoid. Around the middle of 2000, a close friend of mine found himself the focus of an evangelical Christian colleague's attention, who spoke frequently of Islamic extremists in our midst, for her husband worked for the Metropolitan Police force and apparently had much to say about Muslim radicals. Tired of her constant bombardment, my friend asked her to find out why one of those men was still free to preach despite frequent complaints from the Muslim community at large. His question was never answered. To be continually told by the government, media and senior police officers today, therefore, that the Muslim community in Britain is in denial about the existence of extremists amongst us is quite hard for me to grasp. The warnings I received were not from lapsed Muslims who were happy to compromise their beliefs for political gain, but from practising, active individuals. Prior to the destruction of the World Trade Centre on 11 September, 2001, I listened to many Muslims lamenting the authorities' refusal to deal with people well known to be creating community tensions. Indeed, witnessing this laxity, some members of the community even began to entertain conspiracy theories about these free men. The Muslim community complained about their outrageous statements and the authorities appeared to do nothing.

For the first year and a half as a Muslim I enjoyed the company of a small group of friends who were predominantly apolitical *Salafis* who believed that a renewal of an Islamic society lay with the purification of the individual's soul. 'God does not change the condition of a people,' they would often say, quoting the Qur'an, 'until they change the condition of themselves.'[34] Today much is made of the threat that Hizb-ut-Tahir poses to British society, with calls for it to be proscribed arising from various quarters, but this does not marry my experience. My friends certainly derided the group as the Socialist Worker Party for Muslims with its Leninist view that all of the problems of the Muslim world would be solved once the Caliphate was restored, but its members were viewed as an irritant more than a menace. I once encountered an angry scene before a lecture at a mosque during which a *Salafi* seized upon some Hizb-ut-Tahir literature and proceeded to tear them to shreds, complaining that the ideas contained therein were dangerous and heretical, but apart from that I had the impression that very few people took their ideas seriously. A close friend of mine who had started practising Islam just before I became Muslim was swayed by the ideas of this group and so I frequently encountered his arguments in favour of working for the return of Muslim governance, since they believed that the governments of the Muslim world were not Islamic.

Contrary to contemporary claims about violent activism on the part of its members, I found that they were obsessed with the concept of intellectual argument which they seemed to believe would change the world. Their only reference to violence was in their critique of British and US foreign policy, which they viewed as an aggressive force in the Muslim world, detailed in tracts—Socialist Worker style—which they would thrust into the hands of worshipers after every Friday prayer: this was no call to arms for the violence belonged to the West. I never attended any of their meetings, so of course I cannot say what went on behind closed doors. Still, my friends and I tended to think of them as a broken record—a talking shop—harping on and on, and on, about the same issue over and over again at the expense of any spiritual growth. Indeed when I once declined an invitation to join a friend for an evening smoking fruit-flavoured tobacco from a *sheesha* pipe, suggesting that this was perhaps not the way a Muslim should pass his time, he replied that we would adopt this attitude when the Caliphate returned. Until then, it was business as usual. This said it all for me.

I was a great idealist for the first few years as a Muslim, seeing that letter of James come alive in my own life. I got on with the task of adopting Islamic characteristics which mirrored my favourite epistle: quick to listen, slow to speak and slow to get angry; speak and act as men who are judged under a Law which makes them free; if faith does not lead to action, it is itself a lifeless thing; a man who controls his tongue is capable of controlling every part of his body; God opposes the arrogant and gives grace to the humble; a good man's prayer is powerful and effective. Once I had established the prayer and had learnt the foods I could eat, my concern turned to the purification of my heart. According to the Qur'an our success is linked to the purity of our soul:

> By the sun and his brightness, and the moon when she follows him, and the day when it reveals him, and the night when it enshrouds him, and the heaven and Him Who built it, and the earth and Him Who spread it out, and a soul and Him Who perfected it and inspired it with awareness of what is wrong for it and what is right for it, he is indeed successful who purifies it, and he is indeed a failure who neglects it.[35]

Initially my overwhelming concern lay with sincerity. Islam teaches that actions are only accepted according to the intentions that lie behind them: 'Whoever's emigration is for some worldly gain which he can acquire or a woman he will marry,' said our Prophet ﷺ, 'then his emigration is for that which he emigrated.'[36] Sincerity to God is the key to faith in Islam. Believers must ensure that all acts of worship are done exclusively for God's pleasure. Where a person's intention is to show off, their acts of worship may be nullified. The greatest action such as feeding multitudes of the poor could be reduced to nothing because one's intention was to earn a good reputation. Yet at the same time even the smallest action can be made great by the intention behind it. Intention and honesty are intimately linked, and the desire to honour God is tied to both.

When I came to believe in Islam my journey had barely begun. The early days were often characterised by feelings of fear and isolation as I negotiated the reactions of family, friends and even complete strangers. At the same time I discovered that I had greater strength than I gave myself credit for, persevering with my new-found faith and ignoring the disdain of others. Some of the university's non-practising Muslims hypothesised that I had been pressurised to convert by *fundos*, while a group of practising Muslims—questioning my sincerity—agreed that they should view my adoption of Islam with suspicion. The theories of others varied: I wanted an ethnic religion, it was an act of rebellion, I had been pressurised by friends or it was a passing phase. Of all those who had formed an opinion of me and my change, very few ever thought to actually ask me for an explanation and even when I did explain it seemed that they did not believe me. The reality was that a discomfort within— the call of my heart—drove my search for God. It was perhaps only natural then that my first steps as a Muslim centred upon looking inwards as I focused on treating a lump of flesh beneath my ribs.

The testimony of faith signified a new beginning for me, like others before it and others since. Whenever we repent of our sins it is a new beginning, just as it was a new beginning when I started attending church again in my quest for truth. Each new beginning comes after an awakening inside, although change is not always immediate. When I was asked why I had become a Muslim there were many answers I would give: some-times I would say that I had been brought this way through reading, through listening and through watching, but the final impetus was deeper than that. There was that awakening within to the realisation that I needed guidance and had to change. Some months before I became Muslim I spent a bright Saturday morning wandering aimlessly through the streets of London and it was while heading through the Regent's Park that something within troubled me. My response to this was a turning point in which I began to speak to God and made myself a covenant with Him.

Islam is a religion of reform: it refreshes, brings life anew and grants new beginnings. It was clear as I struggled with myself in my new faith that action was required on my part. Belief in itself was not enough, for I had to begin the process of reforming my character. It was not that I was an incredibly bad person who had to go through a complete transformation—I certainly had my share of virtues to help me on my way—but I was aware of a number of issues that required redress. Emerging from a tradition whose entire theology hangs on the idea that mankind is primarily a sinful being in need of salvation it is easy to go to extremes in viewing oneself in a wholly negative light, but many of my concerns were genuine. The majority of them were related to the heart—sincerity, honesty, gratitude, the use of words, suspicion, envy. My pursuit of the outward forms of worship lacked precision as I uncritically absorbed the plentiful but sometimes contradictory advice of well-meaning individuals around me; once I had learned the basics I found that I could not dwell on them any more.

I was never very good at performing the ritual prayers on time and rarely followed them with the optional prayers favoured by my friends, preferring to do the bare minimum in the hope that it would see me through. As my studies in London drew to a close, I began telling myself that I would practice properly once I moved away, escaping the controversies that divided the Muslims at my college. This was not a very logical view for I was about to leave the company of like-minded individuals to spend time with people who disliked Islam. Yet although my practice did not improve over that period, I still encountered moments of renewal prompted by the worries that I faced.

One evening, having applied to study for a post-graduate degree and wondering what my future had in store for me given that I still had not received an offer of a place by mid-summer, I decided to read a prayer known as *istikarah*, which is the supplication for seeking guidance in forming a decision or choosing the proper way. After my main evening prayer, I knelt on my bedroom carpet with my English prayer book in hand and addressed my Lord: if my going to study Publishing was good for me in relation to my religion, my life and end, then decree and facilitate it for me, and if it be ill for me, remove it from me and remove me from it. The very next day I received an offer in the post. Remembering my supplication as I retrieved the envelope from the doormat, my faith was suddenly renewed, it felt strong and I became devoted in my prayers.

This renewal, alas, did not last and I soon returned to my former self. A few weeks later I had an argument with one of my siblings, both of us saying things that would offend the other. I thought that the family conversation about our argument would destroy me for I knew that I would never be asked to explain my side of the story. Descending into misery as the sense of isolation overcame me, I went inside and prayed. After half an hour I felt better and again I was devoted to God for a while.

Throughout the summer, these beginnings recurred, for despite my wavering and the constant struggle that I found myself facing, one thing always seemed self-evident. I knew that if my life were to end suddenly, I would not be ready. This is why I persevered, returning in a hurry to renew my faith after every period of stagnation. Each of us is responsible for the ultimate destination of our soul; no one can believe for us. Between my soul and God, I always remind myself, stand my heart and my deeds, and our end is in our own hands.

There is an undeniable truth which faces us, which is that no excuse will suffice when we confront the Day of Judgement. Through 'negligence, weakness and our own deliberate fault' we sometimes place ourselves in great danger. It is clear that we can conceal the diseases of our hearts from one another, but we realise that on that awesome Day when we gather before our

Lord there will be no cover for them unless we strive to cure them now. Each time I turn back to God in repentance I tell myself that I must hurry to put things right. God is most merciful, nullifying every bad action that passed before whenever we sincerely beg for His forgiveness. Having detailed the consequences of living a sinful life, the Qur'an states: '…except for those who repent, believe and do good deeds. For them does God convert their evil deeds into good. And God is eternally forgiving and merciful.'[37] Ever since I came to believe in Islam these phases of realisation and renewal have accompanied me; they have been the central theme of this journey of mine, characterising my struggle between reconciling my heart and other calls.

This is an intensely personal journey and yet it is not a road that we can travel alone. I will always be grateful to a friend who provided wise counsel whilst I was studying in Scotland and feeling the effects of isolation. I knew of eight practising Muslims on campus whom I sometimes encountered in the prayer room throughout the day, but generally I lacked any kind of spiritual support; indeed the responsibility of organising the Friday prayer, social gatherings and the break of fast in *Ramadan* had been placed upon me, a role I disliked given that I had only recently joined the fold of the faithful and considered myself the one most in need of help. The result was a growing sense of unease, which my friends detected in the emails I regularly dispatched. Unlike those companions who will tell us only exactly what we want to hear, I discovered that I had friends who would always go well beyond the extra mile to help a person in need. One such friend travelled an extra 420 miles north from London to tell me that God had done His part in guiding me: now it was my turn to strive in His way in an effort to repay my debt.

My friend did not tell me what I wanted to hear—I wanted sympathy to support my self-pity—but his words were true all the same. There is indeed so much that I owe my Creator—so much that I cannot innumerate. I am grateful that He granted me my loving, caring parents and I am grateful to them—although they may not think so given that I chose to walk this path, not theirs. But I am grateful; I am grateful for their unerring provision, the clothing they provided for me in my youth, the education they furnished me with and the meals they prepared for me day after day. I am grateful that they sent me to Sunday school and took me to church, and instilled in me my moral compass. I am grateful for all these things and I thank God for granting me bounties greater than I can measure.

I am grateful that He granted me so many friendships throughout my years and throughout this land and others. I am grateful to my Lord for granting me the gift of faith. I am grateful to the Most Merciful for making me shy throughout my youth. I am grateful that He protected me from bringing harm upon myself. I am grateful that He granted me warmth and gave me food. I am grateful that He protected me from harm and has sustained my life long enough for me to begin to correct my conduct and start to purify my heart. I am grateful that God tested me in a way which made me appreciate His bounty. I am grateful that He makes my heart ache whenever I do wrong and that He causes tears to well up in my eyes when I stumble into sin. I am grateful indeed. May God, how glorious is He, forgive me for every moment of sadness, for every moment spent with ingratitude. There is so much that God has poured upon me and I am truly grateful.

In life we must always remind ourselves of the debt we owe our Lord. Seven years ago a flat battery had to remind me this. That morning my rented car would not start and so I had to call out recovery. It was funny how something foreign could become so familiar within such a short space of time, such that something we could once do without becomes something we take for granted. It was funny how when something is always there we do not thank God for it as we do when something new arrives. We pray for safe travels when we go on holiday and thank Him on our arrival, but the daily trip to work and back becomes a routine normality which we do not thank Him for.

We pray for sound employment and thank Him when He responds, but we take our daily bread without the same words of thanks. We ask for good health when struck down with illness and thank Him when we recover, but as we go about our everyday business in good health, sometimes we forget to thank the One who has power over all things.

When I first got that car I was wondering at all the blessings that God had bestowed on me, but soon I would get in the car in the morning, drive to work and park, failing to say my praise in exchange for His blessings, just as I made my sandwiches at lunchtime without saying, 'Thank you Lord,' just as I would wake in the morning without thanking God for the opportunity of another day to better myself, just as I would write a letter without thanking God for giving me sight—and what an amazing thing that is—just as I would take so many things for granted and yet not express my gratitude to the Bestower of all things.

It reminded me of the words of a poet: 'If my thanking God for His blessings is a blessing, then I must thank Him in the same measure again. How can one thank Him save by His grace as time goes on, and life goes by? If a good thing comes, I rejoice heartily; if a bad one comes, I receive a reward. In both cases He gives me a gift too large for the minds of men, and the land and sea.'

That day, I thought, I would not moan about the frost killing my car battery. I decided to thank God instead for giving me time to reflect upon His blessings. How perfect He is, and how we fail to express the gratitude He deserves. Years later it was the sudden beauty of my garden that brought this back to my mind after a seemingly long winter and the arrival of spring at last. Our front garden was suddenly blooming with flushes of new green leaves and splashes of colour everywhere. There were pinkish red flowers on the camellia, purple tulips, bright yellow cowslips, orange on the berberidaceae, yellows, pinks and blues everywhere. The scent was splendid and it was a sight that made me mutter praises of God over and over again.

God has always been generous to me. His magnificence never fails to amaze me. His signs, His bounties and His blessings multiply. One evening I decided to stop writing, for words worry me. The responsibility we shoulder when we use words is great and so that night I decided to rest my pen. Not for the first time, however, I received an email later that evening in which a stranger told me that he found my writing useful. The timing: God's generosity? Why was it that every time I concluded that my writing should cease somebody had words for me? Was it a sign or a test? God knows best, but I know that God is always generous to me. He never ceases to shower His blessings upon me, despite myself. God is great, magnificent.

We say that God is the Most High because everything around us bears witness to this. We say He is Great—*Allahu Akbar*—because this is evident all around us. I thought of His generosity one evening when my computer crashed in the middle of a piece of work. I had spent an hour writing words in my defence, choosing the right words to respond to another's. Yet when I tried to send those words my computer timed out and it timed out three more times after that, and then my other computer crashed when I tried to use it instead. It was then that I recognised God's generosity. What was to be gained by responding? What was to be gained with those words? I recognised His generosity at last, and so finally I deleted that email, wiped away that text and—praise belongs to God—the computer worked once more. God's generosity. Were matters within my hands, were I able to control such things, were I able to decree anything, I would decree that I land face down in the fire of Hell. But God is ever generous, ever protecting us from ourselves, ever granting us an escape from our own wickedness. He is the ever generous, and this is why we call Him the Most High, the Great.

A few days earlier I had been feeling sad and so I returned to my Lord in prayer, supplicating to Him who has the power to grant and withhold. I was feeling confused, recognising that without His help all of us will go astray, and so I prayed as best

I could. What can I say except that God is ever generous? Without any effort on my part, He sends aid, He sends guidance. That day I had conceded that it was time I did the decorating I had been promising my wife all year and so I went down to the hardware store to get some paint. A member of staff there told me that, at last, the Islamic Studies classes were starting in the mosque the following day. He walked with me to the car park and fetched me a timetable from his car. The following morning my wife and I walked the 10-minute trek from our house, across the top of the hill and down through the graveyard to the mosque in that wonderful sunshine for the first class beneath that stunning calligraphy in the dome. The gentle Algerian introduced us to half an hour of Qur'anic commentary and half an hour of the biography of our Prophet ﷺ.

For half an hour he began to tell us the meaning of the Arabic word *hamd*, and for half an hour he described to us the appearance of our blessed Prophet ﷺ. What can one say except that God is the Most Generous, the Most High? What can one say except that we count the Blessings He showers upon us every day?

We learnt that morning that God has said that very few of His servants say *shukr*—thank you—and so we begin every prayer with *Alhamdulilah*, a gift from God, that we thank Him for those things that we are aware of and those things that we are not. *Alhamdulilah*—all praise is for God. God the Most Great saves us from ourselves and gives us the words to say because He knows that we would not say *shukr* on our own accord. *Alhamdulilah*: God is the ever generous.

If I were to write of all the bounties that I felt that weekend it would take up too much space and too much time, but nevertheless I was made aware of His generosity—this was His generosity in itself. I felt humbled and blessed, for God had granted me so much despite myself. He had granted me so much although I am so undeserving. Time after time He protects me from myself and I wish I could repay Him, but I know I never can and so all I can say is this: I seek refuge in

God, the Lord of the Worlds, from myself, and I pray that He guides me and does not let me die other than as one who has earned His pleasure.

In faith I remain an idealist—a literalist to some—who takes the words of the Messenger of God ﷺ to heart. One of the companions of the Prophet ﷺ said, 'I said, "Messenger of God, whose Islam is best?" He said, "The one from whose tongue and hands the Muslims are safe."'[38] Some Muslims mock this simple faith of mine, placing conditions upon those words, loosening the tongue for those perceived to be heretics. Thus disappointment is a word that frequently returns to my mind as I encounter people of knowledge from whose tongues we are not safe, but such feelings can lead to resolve. Though the road will be long and I must forever fight the laziness and distraction that has always accompanied me in life, one day I found my determination to seek true knowledge. In the meantime this simple faith remains with my literal readings of speak good or remain silent; your mother, your mother, your mother; the one from whose tongue we are safe; and this brotherhood of yours is one brotherhood. Fortunately I am not alone in walking this path. A stranger once wrote some words that struck a chord with me:

> For myself, my journey began on these reflections... though blessed with a family and community of Muslims, something was lacking: the frequent quarrels, petty back talking that I witnessed between Muslims and even at the mosque made it obvious that something was missing and soon I was on a search for something greater, and that was the 'Prophetic Character', as I realised that truly that was the foundation of Islam.

He went on:

> So my search began to find the scholars who called to God with the display of the Prophetic character, following

the footsteps of the noble Prophet ﷺ building solid communities based on firm and pure hearts, who went on to call the masses to the religion with the precious light that emitted from the very inner fibres of their beings.

The journey to reconcile oneself with God is ongoing and continuous, and in my case it is one that has only just begun. Though my knowledge now is little, I already know well the gems of the Prophetic character in those few words that I have learned from their renderings into the English language. This is a journey I must undertake myself, for it is my heart and my soul that seeks redemption. I have done the bare minimum for the past few years, but my soul tells me that this is not enough. I do not wish to become a scholar, but merely wish to redeem my soul, to put confusion behind me and to live as our blessed Prophet ﷺ taught us to. I want to live a good life and perhaps—if God wills—embody however faintly the true light of Islam.

I came to Islam towards the end of the 20th century of the Christian era, more than 1,400 years after the Prophet's ﷺ migration to Medina. I came to Islam after the European colonial age which saw the slaughter of Muslim scholars and the Great Powers playing different groups of Muslims off against each other. I came to Islam after the seed of nationalism had grown into a vast but barren tree. I often reflect that those born into practicing Muslim families can at the very least grasp on to the tradition of their parents, seeking refuge in the remains of a living tradition. As converts to Islam we are thrown into the deep sea of confusion, looking this way and that, listening to the competing claims of Muslims here and there. The scholars are the inheritors of the Prophet ﷺ we are told, but perpetually we are warned of corrupt scholars, government scholars, wolves in sheep's clothing and pretenders to the throne. We do not have Muslim heritage to look back on and we cannot ask our grandparents about their grandparents.

Two years ago I found myself harking after the simple faith of the nomad. If I was asked what my creed was, I would only answer with the Prophet's ﷺ words when questioned by the Angel Gabriel, for the frequent, complex debates on the topic meant nothing to me.[39] I prayed, fasted and gave charity, and tried to be kind to those around me. I clung to the community wherever I found myself and focused on those actions about which there is no disagreement: the smile which is a charity, control of the tongue, the five prayers and their companions, a few coins to the one in need and responding to the one who asks.

I could not do more than this, I felt, because my mind was too small to fathom the pathway to the past as it passed through the era of European empire and beyond. An Armenian observer is not alone in her scathing attack on the mischief of the British as they encouraged the Armenian uprising whilst the Turks were defending their borders at the start of the 20th century, for this scene was replicated throughout the colonised lands. Ethnic groups turning on one another, scholars of religion slaughtered and the European powers promoting one group of Muslims against another; the simple faith of the nomad seemed safer somehow.[40]

As an agnostic more than 10 years ago I wrote a somewhat irreverent piece about my search for truth. While I have faith today, testifying that none has the right to be worshipped except God and that Muhammad ﷺ is His messenger, there remains a mustard seed of truth in that piece. For me it is no longer a question of religion, but of navigating the competing claims of self-appointed spokesmen. Just follow the Qur'an and *sunna*, say some, but it is not so simple. There are more than 37,000 *hadith* and more than 6,000 verses of the Qur'an. Am I to interpret them myself given my distance in time, space and language from the Prophet ﷺ and his companions? Muslims agree that the scholars are the inheritors of the religion and best placed to explain these matters to us, but the most vocal commentators insist on warning us of wolves and pretenders to the throne. In reality the Muslim corpus has in place exact sciences to guarantee authenticity—such as the *ijazah* that can be traced to *ijazah*, back through the generations—but there remains a grain of truth in that piece of mine from a decade ago:

> Question everything, but don't tell anyone. When you're on that journey of yours, never confess that you're completely lost. Just smile, grin, and bear it. It's going to infuriate you, but nobody will understand. In their control rooms, they have their timetables and maps. To them it's obvious, so why can't you see that?
>
> …Recently, you were going to church every Sunday, hoping a sermon would cure your questioning mind. And one day, your lucky day, they invite the unsure, the faithless, the agnostic, to stay behind after the service, where they'll explain it to you and make you see the truth. You sit there and wait: you pray they'll make you see, but soon you discover that it's not you who's blind. The preacher arrogantly assumes that you're just ignorant, that you don't have faith because you're ignorant. Because you didn't read the Bible.
>
> 'Well, actually, I was reading the Bible, I just didn't see the proof.'
>
> And what is the preacher's proof? He says it's obvious. Well, no, it isn't obvious, because you wouldn't be sitting here listening to him if it was. He arrogantly assumes that those without faith simply have no faith because they never tried and never thought about it. He tells you that it's obvious, so obvious that even a four year old could understand. But wait. You're not four years old; the four year old didn't read the Bible, she just sucked on her lolly and never wondered if the sugar would rot her teeth.

Yet there is an antidote: I have long noticed how love for the Prophet ﷺ permeates the actions of those who sit and learn and who immerse themselves in learning. Noting how distant I am from that example, I found that their love inspired me to learn, for I have the faith of the nomad, but I want so much more. Taking stock of the longing of my heart, I once came across some more words that resonated with me. It was an article in which the author had written about what traditional Islam meant to him. Part of that description included this sentiment: 'It is the Islam of the quaint villages...'

It reverberated in my mind because for weeks I had been thinking of a faraway place I passed through the previous summer. It also touched me because there is a part of me which does not sit well with the modern age. Throughout my teenage years I was something of an eccentric. While my friends were interested in mountain bikes, football, Nintendo and Baywatch, I was a dreamer. I yearned after a romantic past, of a wood-framed house surrounded by the cottage garden, of self-sufficiency, spring-fed waters, of the homestead farm. I would sketch out my rough architectural diagrams of my self-build Tudor house. My favourite book as a child was Laura Ingalls Wilder's *Farmer Boy*: I imagined I was Almanzo and I dreamed of living my life as he had all those years ago. Later—and this led to my eventual arrival as a student of Development—my attention turned to sub-Saharan Africa. An article about life in Burkina Faso offered me unimaginable inspiration.

Though through marriage and good fortune I now have an extended family whose members include those that live a subsistence lifestyle—residing in wood-framed houses on homestead farms fed by spring waters—with the wisdom of age I realise that all those dreams were indeed for a romantic past. The reality of life is that it is hard: inoculated from birth against mumps and rubella, and against tetanus, living in an age protected from TB, and able to access an education from the age of five to 21, we forget the realities of existence in different times and places.

Still, that was my dream and an element of it remains with me even today. Something was bothering my heart and that article gave me an inkling of what it was: a kind of discomfort with the age we are living in.

One summer I spent two weeks up in the highlands of eastern Turkey with my mother-in-law, up above the clouds. My wife's family originate in Hopa on the Black Sea, close to the border with Georgia in Artvin province. Every year, to escape the summer heat, my mother-in-law packs up her possessions like the nomads of old and ascends the mountains for the refuge of that usually cooler air. Life up there is quite primitive: the houses are simple stone-walled structures without cement, covered with the tarpaulin these travellers bring with them. The evening meal is prepared on wood burning stoves, which in turn warms the shelter as the cold evening draws in.

That August my wife and I began the journey in the early morning one Friday, looking forward to our reunion with her mother after such a long time. There is a vast dam-building project under way in the valley between our village just inland from Hopa and the major town of Artvin, so we had to leave at first light so we could travel while the road along the bottom of the valley was still open. We travelled inland rising steadily higher and higher into the mountains. At around 11 in the morning we stopped in Ardanuç to get some vegetables and have a rest, but not for too long. Soon we were winding up a dirt track through a beautiful landscape which reminded me of my holidays in Switzerland as a child. It was a steep landscape of meadows, streams and log chalets. It was a landscape that almost made me cry tears of joy. We were heading for a *yayla* about two hours short of Ardahan, but I could have stopped just there, so magnificent was the scenery.

We continued onwards however until we came to a camping ground on the side of a valley, where we stopped for lunch. There was a shack on the edge in which a group of men were preparing to barbeque cubes of lamb meat. I sat down on a bench with the lady-folk close to an ice-cold spring, for we had just discovered that the men were chilling bottles of Turkish spirits beneath the bubbling surface. After lunch, leaving my male travelling companions to their Raki and the ladies to their conversation, I caught a lift with an old Muslim man back to the mosque for the Friday prayer. I speak very little Turkish, but that ride was an immense blessing: we exchanged *salams* and I watched as those I had left behind appeared as dots across the valley.

This trip to the mosque had been in my thoughts for many weeks, and made the words about the Islam of the quaint villages strike such a chord with me. I should think that mosque had never seen an English Muslim enter its doors in all its ancient history. We parked our car just off the road, because the mosque could only be reached on foot. Together, communicating with one another only by hand gestures and that brotherly fondness in our hearts, we walked up the hill through that village that seemed to be caught in a time warp. There was a water-trough fed by a stream in front of the mosque—what a beautiful sight—but it was the sight in the small garden in front of that place of prayer that touched my heart. All of the men were gathered in a circle, awaiting the call to prayer, expressing such affection for one another, conversing with kind words. We exchanged *salams*, but I did not join them, entering the mosque instead with my old companion. That building seemed centuries old inside. It was dark, and yet it seemed light. The walls were stone, not decorated like those fine mosques of Istanbul. There were some pieces of calligraphy high up on the walls and old worn out rugs on the floor. There was a spirit in that mosque which warmed my soul. This was the place that occupied my thoughts.

The tale of the remainder of my journey up into the mountains is for another time. This story is about that place in my heart. It is not a geographical space, but an emotional place. That place that the author described: 'It is the Islam of the quaint villages…' Yes, this is the yearning of my heart. That place of true brotherhood outside the mosque, that place of a simplicity that does not care for our modern-day obsessions with labels and debates. That place where God is remembered, where life stops for the prayer, where brothers respect one another and welcome the stranger passing through. That place of beauty.

CHAPTER FOUR

Obstacles To Our Dreams

Our dreams—the yearnings of our heart—are the antidote to the wild world in which we live today. The discomfort with the age we are living in is real, but it is unavoidable all the same. The Prophet ﷺ informed his followers that a time would come when holding on to religion would be like holding on to hot coals—a metaphor that increasingly strikes true with every passing day.[41] There often appears to be no beauty—no mercy, no goodness, no light—in the behaviour of people of religion, while irreligious folk claim the high moral ground, sometimes justifiably. The apparent confounds those sincere men and women attracted to faith who must forever negotiate accusation and association, navigating arduous hurdles towards their goal. Extremism has become the order of the day—from the religious and irreligious in equal measure—setting in place great obstacles to our dreams. 'When elephants fight,' went a Swahili proverb I encountered during my travels in Tanzania a decade ago, 'it is the grass that gets crushed'.

One day the Prophet ﷺ informed his followers, 'Extremists shall most certainly perish,' repeating these words three times.[42] These are the days when decent and honourable people must express respect for one another as we witness nations gathering to devour the weak just as people share a plate of food.[43] In the name of human rights, human rights are abused. In the name of freedom, innocent men and women are incarcerated. In the name of religion, believers are cut down with Kalashnikov rifles and explosive belts. In the name of civilisation, vacuum bombs, cluster bombs and cruise missiles are rained down on far-off lands. Insignificant though they may seem, our dreams and our actions are the antidote—the quiet counter-revolution—to the anarchy unfolding around us.

Conflict

In August 1998, three months after I became Muslim, hundreds of civilians were killed when simultaneous bombs exploded in the capitals of Tanzania and Kenya. Three years later we would witness two commercial jets slamming into the World Trade Centre in New York on our television screens. In each case the perpetrators are thought to have been Muslim and the spectre of a violent religion has been with us ever since. With every passing year, the picture only becomes gloomier as even the gentlest believer is charged with explaining the brutality of the world in which we live. A stranger once sent me a message in which he complained that a tenet of my religion is working to conquer every land on earth.

A tenet is a central principle or belief and so his accusation threw me for this is not one of either the six articles of belief or the five pillars of faith. The Six Articles are belief in God; in all the Prophets and Messengers sent by God; in the Books sent by God; in the Angels; in the Day of Judgement and our Resurrection; and in divine decree. The five pillars of Islam are the profession of faith in God; establishing the five daily prayers; the paying of alms to be distributed amongst the poor; fasting in the month of *Ramadan*; and the pilgrimage to Mecca. Naturally our practices number many more than this, but they cannot be said to be tenets.

I have never been one to view the Muslim world through rose-tinted spectacles, nor have I shied away from condemning the violence and depravity emerging from Muslim lands. I dislike the refrain that the West is to blame for the state of Muslim countries, for although those who study history and politics may see a shadow of truth in this, the full picture is infinitely complex. The reason for my reservations lies in my faith, for blaming others is not a Muslim tradition: the Qur'an recounts the lessons of the Children of Israel—the Muslims of that age— precisely so that we may not repeat the mistakes of those who passed before us. Still, I have met Muslims who consider themselves the Chosen People, who look upon others with contempt, considering their lives worthless like Gentiles deserving of whatever they get, although they would never think to share their faith—thus English Muslims are not greeted with joy, but with suspicion and disbelief instead.

'I agree that the Muslim world is awash with violence and depravity, but...' I once experimented with an internet search engine, first typing in the word 'Muslim' and then the word 'Islam'. I cannot report that anything positive came back amidst the first 10 pages. All across the internet, people are writing about the barbarity of Islam—out there, Islam and Muslims are viewed with greater contempt than I could ever have imagined.

While undertaking this exercise I came across an article by a military man stationed at Pearl Harbor in the United States, which argued that the problem is not with the extremists, but with Islam itself. He cited a horrific case in which the so-called religious police had prevented 15 schoolgirls from escaping a burning school dormitory in Mecca because they were not 'properly dressed'. It was the author's opinion that because Islam mandates a certain dress-code these people were correct according to their religion in preventing the children from escaping, which thus proved that Islam is a barbaric religion. Yet if this were true, would Islam not prohibit a person facing starvation from eating *haram* meat in the absence of a substitute?[44]

While I cannot deny that the house of Islam is far from tidy today, I had to object. The author called Islam a barbaric, bloodthirsty and violent religion. Although this description would sadly suit too many Muslims in the world today, I detected hypocrisy. Are those that passionately worship their nation, believing that they stand at the pinnacle of civilisation, free of the same charge?

Do those who describe my religion as barbaric, blood-thirsty and violent not see barbarism everywhere as I do?

The nation whose scientists invented the nuclear bomb was not a Muslim nation. The nation that used the nuclear bomb, the combined death toll of which is estimated to have ranged from 100,000 up to 220,000 of whom most were civilians, was not a Muslim nation. The nation that created and deployed jellied gasoline as a weapon of war—a substance formulated to burn at a specific rate and adhere to material and personnel—was not a Muslim nation: it was Germany for those who will point their fingers at the United States of America. The nation whose engineers invented the vacuum bomb which causes its victims to implode was not a Muslim nation. The nation that used experimental weapons in Iraq such as the high-energy chemical laser was not a Muslim nation. The nation that undertook the extermination of up to six million Jews over a period of five years was not a Muslim nation. The nation that developed Botox and Anthrax as weapons of mass destruction was not a Muslim nation. I could go on.

I see barbarism everywhere in this depraved age of ours. Muslim terrorists have hijacked and blown up civilian airliners, but so have nationalists, socialists and indeed states. In 1988 a US Navy vessel shot down an Iranian passenger jet killing all 290 people on board, while in 1983 the US accused the Soviet Union of shooting down a Korean airliner, killing 269 people. What can we say? Perhaps it is our mindset which is at fault, conditioned by the bloodiest century ever.[45] What can be said of a race—the human race—which has turned killing into a form of entertainment? Today's film industry built upon brutality pales beside the Roman spectacle of gladiators slaying one another, but its existence is no less shocking. We have got death and destruction down to a fine art: the subtle thriller about the lone murderer, the action-packed adventure of one man verses the terrorists complete with buildings exploding and planes crashing, and the grim horror about the obsessed mass murderer: all in the name of entertainment.

The truth makes us weep, for we live in a barbaric and depraved age. We see the kidnappings in Iraq today, but we recall the kidnappings of African-Americans in 1960s America. We see the beheadings of innocents today, but we recall the hangings and lynching of innocents yesterday. We think of the bombs on the London transport system, but we remember the Omagh bombing as well. We lament the bombing of a mosque in Pakistan, but we remember the Oklahoma bombing a decade ago. We see churches destroyed in Indonesia, but we recall the mosques demolished in Bosnia. If we are honest, we see the depravity everywhere: if we remember, if we think deeply.

Yet we remember too that we are not all killing each other, we are not all involved and we do not all have blood on our hands. There is light and love in the world. Consider the Muslim doctor who will see us when we end up in casualty, the Christian nurse who will tend our scars, the aid workers tending to those in need or the man who sees to it that his neighbour is in good health. Despite the depravity, there is still hope. As one of the parables of the Christian gospels tells us, if we remove the plank from our own eyes, we might just find that our appreciation of reality will improve.

We live in a world of cliché in which we lazily recycle the words of others. When it is said that Islam was spread by the sword, it is known to be a trite expression, but nobody cares: it is a slogan. An Afrocentric collector of pottery who knew I was Muslim once seized on a book I was reading about the earliest followers of Jesus ﷺ. 'Nike-ear, nice-eya,' he began, struggling to pronounce probably the most famous council in the history of the Christian Church as he eyed my notes before me: 'Nicewhat? I've never heard of it.' He went on to tell me that the followers of Jesus ﷺ did not accept Islam when it came to their lands: 'It was spread by the sword,' he told me, 'Spread by the sword, my friend.'

It was not clear at the time why he had to make this point, given that my reading material concerned Jews who accepted Jesus ﷺ as the Messiah whilst maintaining their Jewish identity, but often it is interruptions such as these which inspire greater contemplation on topics we might otherwise pass over. If Islam has preserved the character of Jewish Christianity in its teachings, was it perhaps possible that the followers of those sects that came to be seen as heretical as the Church adapted to the influx of Gentile converts actually found their home in Islam? My assailant's words prompted me to ponder on what became of the now heretical sects and to reflect on the survival of the Coptic, Maronite, Melkite, Jacobite and Eastern Orthodox churches, whose followers still worship in Muslim lands today.

My Afrocentric companion was not alone in addressing me with words about violence, however. A Jewish friend upon discovering that I was Muslim during my postgraduate studies exclaimed: 'But you have the whole *jihad* thing.' I considered it strange that a person who had carried a machine gun during her own service in a foreign army could address me in this way, but over the years I have grown used to these odd inter- rogations. A dear relative never tires of condemning Muslim violence in my presence, hoping that I will reflect and see the error of my ways.

My detractors argue that Islam should be considered untrue because of the intolerance and violence exhibited in many parts of the Muslim world today. For my well-meant Christian relative, history must prove rather problematic in this regard. While it may be possible to claim that contemporary English Christians are model citizens—living under the protection of a secular state that controls the eighth most powerful army in the world—many examples of Christian power are hardly flattering. If my faith should be lambasted on the basis of intolerance in some societies today, should Christianity then be held as untrue because of its intolerance in centuries past? Although it is legitimate to argue that aberrations such as Adolf Hitler were not Christians—he may have defined himself this way in public prior to the second world war, but mad man is preferred—it is rather difficult to take this line in relation to bishops and popes. In 1454CE, for example, Pope Nicholas V gave Alfonso V of

Portugal the right to 'invade, search out, capture, vanquish, and subdue all Saracens and pagans whatsoever, and other enemies of Christ wherever they live'.[46]

In truth, we need not delve back into the distant past or far from home to witness stark examples of Christian violence or appeasement of violence. Prominent ministers of the Serbian Orthodox Church were complicit in the former during the Bosnian war of the 1990s, while members of the Church of England are tainted with the latter. Although the war was portrayed at the time as an ethnic conflict—but for the spectre of Islamic extremism famously invoked by the Conservative government as its reason for non-intervention—historians now recognise the role that religion played in this shameful episode of recent European history. The massacre of an estimated 8,000 Muslim men in Srebrenica in July 1995 is only the most famous case amidst a horrific catalogue of abuse. Michael Sells wrote:

> The violence in Bosnia was a religious genocide in several senses: the people destroyed were chosen on the basis of their religious identity; those carrying out the killings acted with the blessing and support of Christian church leaders; the violence was grounded in a religious mythology that characterized the targeted people as race traitors and the extermination of them as a sacred act.[47]

When the Greek Orthodox synod awarded Radovan Karadzic the Order of St Denys of Xante—its highest honour—in the midst of the ethnic cleansing, the evangelical Anglican Bishop of Barking, Roger Sainsbury, was a lone voice in the Church of England in offering condemnation, even as the Greek bishops described Karadzic as 'one of the most prominent sons of our Lord Jesus Christ'.[48] For the Church of England, the spirit of ecumenism appeared to carry greater import than human life, as it sought to maintain positive relations with Orthodox members of the World Council of Churches. The Catholic theologian, Professor Adrian Hastings, wrote in *The Guardian* at the time:

> Reflecting on the response of the churches in Britain
> and within the Ecumenical Movement to Bosnia once
> more, I remain appalled by how little they have done at
> the level of their leadership to recognise without ambi-
> guity what has been happening, to condemn what is evil
> and above all to offer any significant support to a European
> nation oppressed in a way unprecedented since 1945.[49]

What can be said of the former spiritual head of 77 million
worshippers—who only a few years later would demand that
Pakistani Muslims exhibit the tolerance of the Christians—
given his failure to meet his Muslim counterpart in Bosnia
during the war? What can be said of one who has made much
of his role in inter-faith dialogue since his retirement—stating
that the events of 11 September, 2001, and their aftermath gave
new impetus to dialogue between Muslims and Christians[50]—
when many can only recall how he stumbled at an hour of great
need less than a decade earlier? Much is made of the Muslim
predicament in light of the terrorist atrocities in 2001, but most
prefer to forget the great crime of Srebrenica in 1995 and the
appeasement of the Church along the road that led there. In
truth, Christian involvement in violence is as shameful as the
Muslim's.

Should we expect Christians to abandon their faith because
of the violence and intolerance exhibited in the past and in
other parts of the world today? Should proud atheists abandon
their position based on the behaviour of communist regimes?
Should ardent secularists search their souls concerning the role
of the military in enforcing secular values on religious pop-
ulations in many parts of the world today? Are they useful
criteria for determining truth? I did not adopt Islam on a whim
of fashion or for social convenience; thus questions about the
terrible way Muslims behave prove irrelevant.

What a religion itself teaches in relation to these matters is
important however, and so Muslims are fortunate to find that
the orthodox position is clear. Muslims soldiers, for example,

are expected to observe strict codes of conduct and sophisticated rules of engagement in war, defined from within the faith not without. While Islam acknowledges that warfare is an unfortunate characteristic of human societies, it does not recognise the concept of total war—in which innocent civilians may be killed and their property destroyed—but only allows warfare if it is a means of limiting greater harm. 'And fight for the sake of God those who fight you,' says the Qur'an, addressing those in authority, 'but do not commit excesses, for God does not love those who exceed the Law.'[51] Peace is preferred to war, however: 'Now if they incline toward peace, then incline to it, and place your trust in God.'[52] The scholars of Islam have always held that a Qur'anic verse that ordered the Muslims to fight the idolaters referred to a specific historical episode in which the Meccan Confederates had breached the Treaty of Hudaybiyya and that no legal rulings could be derived from the verse on its own.[53] Even if this were not the case, they state that its interpretation would still be dependent on other indicators, in which case it could only refer to a situation during a valid war where no ceasefire has been declared.

A famous *hadith* records that 'The best *jihad* is a true word in the face of a tyrannical ruler.'[54] Islamic law states that a Muslim soldier may not kill any women or child-soldiers unless they are in direct combat and then only in self-defence, and all other non-combatants are included in this prohibition. There is no legal justification for circumventing this convention in Islamic law and any such action is defined both as *haram* and a major sin. Furthermore, the decision and right to declare war does not lie with an individual—even if he is a scholar or a soldier—but only with the executive authority of the state. Under Islamic law the ends can never justify the means unless the means are in themselves permissible.[55]

A thought occurred to me one morning whilst listening to the radio in my car: do suicide bombers pray *istikarah*—the prayer in which we ask that God guides us towards that which is best for us. We had just heard a report from Baghdad which detailed yet more civilian deaths. When we pray *istikarah*, truly consigning the matter to God and suspending our own inclinations, Muslims believe that God will make events unfold in the direction that is the best for our worldly and religious affairs. Given that orthodoxy considers suicide bombing *haram* I imagined the individual intent on this course of action being arrested shortly after praying *istikarah*, or falling down a hole, oversleeping or dying before ever getting as far as carrying out the act. My blurted-out question pales into insignificance of course, once we read what the orthodox scholars of Islam say about suicide bombing. Prior to the most recent war in Iraq, the Marxist-Leninist Tamil Tigers were responsible for more such bombings than any other organisation. Amongst those that carried out suicide bombings during the campaign against French, American and Israeli targets in Lebanon in the 1980s were Christians and members of secular leftist groups such as the Communist party. When the Palestinian group Hamas adopted this practice in 1994, many jurists of Islamic law immediately sought to make clear that such actions were indefensible.[56]

Nevertheless, I am frequently reminded of violence apparently conducted in the name of Islam. A work colleague approached me early one morning and asked me to explain how young people could be persuaded to take their own lives by older people who clearly had no intention of giving up their own. Naturally I could not help him with his enquiry, but still he continued to probe me on the spectre of a group of newly religious men disembarking from a train at London's King's Cross with rucksacks packed with explosives strapped to their backs. It was not enough for me to disown terrorism and its perpetrators: because I share a faith with a group of men who did not return home on 7 July, 2005, I must face an inquisition which demands answers to questions I do not understand.

Everybody has their own story to accompany the events of that sunny day in July and I remember my experience well. After the commotion of the morning, I was asked to attend a meeting with my manager during which we intended to discuss the implementation of a national computer system in our GP practices. I was with my colleagues at first, but soon my mind began to wander. I was sitting at the back of that now mangled bus. I was on my way to work, minding my own business, lost in my own world. There was a bag left underneath my seat. I looked to my left and right, I assumed it belonged to one of my fellow passengers, but I did not ask them. Perhaps they were wondering the same thing, but we all kept our minds on our own business, the way we always do. I was not in my meeting now: my colleagues were speaking but I did not hear them. Instead I was in that bus and it suddenly exploded and what was the end for me? I felt sick. I could see those poor souls as their bodies were torn to shreds by a bomb beneath the seat: their last moment gone before they could even see it coming. The shock jolted me back to my meeting. I was supposed to be taking notes, but I had missed the conversation. Did the people who did this never visualise that moment as I did in my meeting, I wondered? Did they never imagine this scene when they planted their bombs? Could they have done this if they had? I felt as though I was going to vomit, but I blocked it from my mind: back to our ill-fated computer system. When we left the room at the end of the meeting, we were told that our organisation was no longer on standby to receive the mass evacuation of casualties. We had officially been stood down. The crisis was over for us, but I still felt nauseous.

That evening my wife was stranded in London as public transport ground to a halt and had gone to wait with a friend. I left home at half past eight finding clear roads all the way, from this hilly valley to those towers of concrete. Indoors, eyes were glued to television screens and few cars passed me all the way. I arrived at 9.20pm just in time for the evening prayer, gliding through the ghost town. I told my friend that I was disgusted by all this—I said that I knew our thoughts should be with the victims, but I could not help praying that the perpetrators were anarchists or something. My friend said they were—

but he was using it as an adjective, while I wanted it to be the noun. In the Name of God, the Most Gracious, Most Merciful: if only we dwelled on this. Would there then be any of this chaos? In the Name of God, not in my name or yours. If we truly reflected, would men of religion cut down innocents with explosives, thinking their deeds are good?

A week later our organisation chose to observe two minutes' silence collectively, standing in the blazing sunshine in the car park outside our office. I felt sad and distant from my colleagues at the time, for I would listen as they spoke of this event momentarily, only to find that the happy, jolly mood prevailed as if nothing of significance had happened. That day I hated some of my friends as they stood out in the car park, laughing and joking merrily right up until the clock struck twelve. There were two minutes without words—although all the cars but one continued their journeys onwards—but as soon as the two minutes were up, a bunch of fools burst into laughter at the hilarity of their self-centred discussions.

I returned inside in silence, lamenting the hideous hypocrisy. For the past week I had been wandering around in a daze, fearing that the Muslim's time in this country was up, that we had reached the end of the road: the Reichstag had been torched, thus the pogroms would begin. Looking around me, however, I doubted this now, for these people were indifferent *in extremis*. Life in the *Big Brother* household was the greater concern in my office. Two days after the bombings, I had journeyed to a meeting in East London where I found myself remarking to my wife that the residents did not look sad at all. Quite the contrary: it was business as usual with smiles on a thousand faces. Journalists were defining the mood as a nation getting on with life as normal in defiance, but indifference seemed a more accurate description to me.

As we stood in the car park at midday on 14 July, 2005, we all witnessed the real display of dignity. A Muslim taxi driver had stopped his car just on the roundabout and now stood with his head bowed next to his door in the middle of the road. There he remained for the next two minutes as the traffic worked around him: an island amidst the chaos.

Whilst staying in Turkey barely a month after those hideous events, it became apparent that the loss of British life was only considered a tragedy if it was a means of scoring points against Islam. If ever we were unfortunate enough to mention our faith or to walk to the mosque for prayer, our socialist companions would remind us of what had happened that fateful day and who was behind it. I would respond by pointing out that the leftist Kurdistan Workers' Party blew up British citizens only a few days later, but apparently this would not be condemned with the same ferocity—instead they were silent. Much was being made of the bombings in the Turkish press for it suited their agendas like it did our companions'—they suffered from selective sympathy and the inability to harbour equal sorrow for all victims of violence.

In making their cheap political jibes they forgot that Britons had experienced 30 years of terrorism at the hands of the IRA and that Londoners were the target of a white supremacist who planted nail bombs in the hope of sparking a race war much more recently. Were the lives of the victims of these attacks worth less because the perpetrators happened not to be Muslim? They also ignored the fact that July marked the 60th anniversary of nuclear bombs being dropped on Hiroshima and Nagasaki, and the tenth anniversary of the slaughter of thousands of Muslims in Srebrenica.

Are Muslims peculiar amongst humanity as perpetrators of extreme violence? The answer is no, of course; the last century and the beginning of the present one have been marked by extreme violence—wars on massive scales, the development of the most terrifying weapons ever conceived, the extermination of whole peoples, torture and terrorism. If the lives of all innocents killed in this chaotic madness are not considered to be of equal worth regardless of who they are or who killed them, we ourselves begin to slide into complicity. Our horror, sorrow and anger no longer stem from our reaction to the inhumanity of others, but from on whose side we find ourselves. I wished that the Turkish chauvinists would reflect on this.

I have never been a good believer, neither as a Christian before those six years of agnosticism nor as a Muslim ever since. My faith has never been zealous; when I said I did not believe in God from the age of 15 even my atheism was agnostic. Nevertheless, however simple my faith may be, I do tend to take words seriously. I waver and slip often, sometimes steaming off as if towards oblivion, but those short Semitic sayings always call me back before long.

My literal interpretation of gospel advice to turn the other cheek meant that I would rarely stand up for myself if I was picked on at school—it was a revelation for me when a family member asked me why not in my final year of junior school. We were brought up on the good book, attending church and Sunday school throughout childhood, and the earliest of those snippet teachings remain with me. I suppose it is this simple, literal faith of mine which leaves me so disappointed with the world we live in: we—believers of all faiths—are taught one thing, but then told to do something else according to the circumstances in which we find ourselves.

I am not under any illusions about the conflicts defining modern-day Britain—the most vocal voices define us as a secular nation, while traditionalists maintain this is a Christian land— but one can still dream that something of our religious heritage might shine through and colour the way we treat one another. Just imagine what public life would be like if it were defined by the citizen's faith rather than a bizarre Machiavellian world-view. How would all this public calling-Muslims-to-account look in the light of words their saviour is said to have uttered?

> How can you say to your friend, 'Brother, let me remove the speck that is in your eye,' when you yourself do not see the plank that is in yours? Hypocrite! First remove the plank from your own eye, and then you will see clearly to remove the speck that is in his.[57]

There is no denying that we Muslims are falling far short of our ideals in our personal and political relationships, but it is gross hypocrisy for British politicians and the press to demand that we get our house in order whilst they themselves are falling short. The Muslim community in Britain is a tiny minority making up 2.7 per cent of the population and a disparate group made up of many ethnicities and following numerous inter-pretations of Islam. Finding myself reading about Camp Xray, Abu Ghraib prison and the cost of the war in Iraq various truths dawned on me. It is in no way reassuring, but it remains the case that conflict and brutality are not the preserve of any particular group. Wherever the heart of man is diseased, his actions respond accordingly. 'A good tree,' we remind ourselves, 'cannot produce bad fruit, nor can a bad tree produce good fruit.'[58]

Extremism

Repeatedly over recent years, newspapers and broadcasters have labelled as extremists people whom many Muslims consider to be voices of moderation. Week after week, just before the radio phone-in host denounces the alleged actions of another extremist amongst us, we hear that tired refrain: 'The vast majority of Muslims are peaceful people...' But who are the vast majority of Muslims and what do they believe? How are they defined and who defined them? In many senses I find my belief in Islam a continuation of my upbringing, not a rejection of it, and I have hardly suffered an identity crisis because of my beliefs. Yet with the use of undefined phrases such as 'the vast majority' and 'moderate Muslims', and the claims that are made on their behalf, our place in society does seem to be in question. But perhaps we are not the first group of people to have experienced this, as a wiser Muslim noted.[59]

Not even a century ago, Jews were forced by the frenzy of state and media to debate their place in society; would it be integration or isolation, tradition or reform? Were they moderates, or fanatics obsessed with a law which should have no place in a modern secular society? Today, for all the lessons that were supposed to have been learned from history, little has changed. Like the good moderate Jews before us, we too must become secular. If not, then once more the talk will be of parasites on society, of an ungrateful community burdened by their religious law and plotting the nation's downfall from ghettoes in its midst.

Too often, discussion about Islam starts, and sometimes finishes, with the topic of fundamentalism, writing off any dimension of spirituality amongst the community's faithful in the process. Generous authors often concede that fundamentalism is common to all faiths, but it must be acknowledged that what is meant in each case is actually very different. In the Christian context it is generally used to signify conservative Protestantism characterised by a literal interpretation of the Bible as God's unadulterated word. In the case of Islam, by contrast, all orthodox Muslims believe the Qur'an to be the word of God, but the term fundamentalist is not generally used in this sense. Instead it is more often aligned with ideas of extreme militancy, although this too is dependent upon the intention of the one who is wielding the label.

As in any scientific tradition, what is meant by a term must be specified from the outset. If Muslim fundamentalism is viewed in the same light as conservative Protestantism it becomes not a radical reaction against other forces, but merely a manifestation of accepted dogma. However this is clearly not what is meant; the idea of Muslim fundamentalism has entirely different connotations.

We are not witnessing different expressions of the same concept, but rather different concepts given a single name. One author has a definition of fundamentalism as 'the conviction that the authentic version of their faith is to be found in the earliest period'.[60] We might say that this best describes the common ground for the term when used for both Christianity and Islam.

In the community in which I live there is a significant problem of extremism amongst sections of the Muslim youth, but it is the extreme of not knowing Islam or not following its teachings, rather than the mode depicted most commonly. In this community, our concerns are with drug use, alcohol addiction and anti-social behaviour. A friend tells me that some young British-Pakistanis are bringing drugs into the area to foster a previously non-existent trade in the town. Our local press has reported on young people being given *Anti-Social Behaviour Orders* on a number of occasions; troublingly in each case the recipients have had Muslim names. Late on Friday and Saturday nights, young British-Pakistanis gather in the centre of town, smoking perpetually and ranting aggressively with sentences littered with expletives. This is probably not what the middle-class commentators have in mind when they call for Muslims to integrate with society; still here the Muslims certainly are adopting the culture of those they find themselves amongst.

Undoubtedly, where it exists, British Muslims have a duty to tackle the commonly defined form of extremism in our midst, but there is also an urgent need to tackle the vast array of social problems which have emerged in areas of deprivation. A friend of mine was until recently the head of department in an inner city London secondary school and he was often appalled by the behaviour of many of his students—more so, he lamented, because the majority of them had Muslim backgrounds. Apart from having no knowledge of their religion whatsoever, many of these young people lacked manners, appeared to have no respect for the people around them and were frequently members of gangs.

The Muslim community makes up barely two per cent of the British population and yet seven per cent of the prison population. According to the *Muslim Youth Helpline* mental illness occurs more frequently amongst Muslim youth than any other group, particularly in the case of those that enter Britain as refugees. Almost half of *Muslim Youth Helpline* clients complain of mental anxiety, depression or suicidal feelings.

For several years I worked with a national helpline charity which aimed to help Muslim women in crisis. As in wider society, domestic violence is rife, divorce rates are high and the issue of forced marriage persists. It is sad to report that a high number of unwanted babies are being abandoned by Muslims in the care of social services, most often by those who become pregnant outside marriage. Meanwhile educational achievement amongst a large segment of the Muslim population remains poor. All in all, as a community we have huge problems and the question of militant extremism is only one of many.

When our former prime minister addressed the Muslim community on the topic of doing more to tackle extremism, the first response was naturally one of defence. We asked what power we have, given that the extremist groups quite deliberately do not frequent established mosques. If wider British society is understandably not asked to root out the extremism of the BNP, we asked, why should the Muslims be charged with taking on the role of the police and local government? Once these initial objections passed, we were faced with a very uncomfortable truth: despite pockets of light—and there are many examples of the Muslim community making a positive and successful con-tribution to society—there are issues which we as a community seriously need to address.

Merely resorting to a very un-Islamic sense of victimhood is not going to help any of us. Merely condemning terrorism is not going to benefit us either, nor is my writing about social ills. Like my friends who went into teaching and youth support work, or those running the various community helplines, there is a realisation that we need to get out into the community to engage in social works. It is time that we awoke to the realities facing us. As we move on after the massacre on the London transport system in 2005, the focus on the Muslim community will no doubt intensify. Some of it will be unfair, some of it deeply insulting, some of it untrue, but Muslims must not pity themselves for we have a lot of work to do. If one of you sees something bad, our religion teaches us, you should change it with your hands, and if you cannot do that you should change it with your tongues, and if you cannot do that you should hate it in your heart, and that is the weakest of faith.

What of the phenomenon of political extremism? Alas, if we are honest, it is not difficult to appreciate how radicalisation might occur in individuals of any community. One day I had the misfortune to watch the previous evening's edition of *Newsnight* and was thus bombarded with the disgusting images that were just emerging from Abu Ghraib prison in Iraq, that I had so far managed to avoid. In my case, I found that the sense of frustration and powerlessness in the face of such inhumanity heightened my emotions so that I began to mull over how we should respond. Some of those ideas surprised me. When my wife asked me to supplicate to our Lord after our evening prayer on behalf of the victims, I was lost for words: I did not know what to pray. My wife told me that prayer is the weapon of believers, but a sense of despair blanked my mind. Against a backdrop of that sense of futility and despair, an action normally considered extreme might start to settle in the mind as the only viable alternative to doing nothing.

I believe I live a fairly sheltered existence given my deliberate abstention from watching television. I know the power of the moving image well—it grips us and etches itself on the mind. Having seen those images and checked my own reaction, it was not difficult to imagine the likely affect on a young man constantly exposed to the drip-drip of brutality represented on his television channels, be it the violence of occupation or the cruelty of terrorism. As for those who experience such things first hand, I wonder how they could not react in the manner we all condemn; only those with the greatest faith could surely withstand the abuse perpetuated against them and their people, whoever they are and wherever they are from. I found that incredibly sad at the time, for a voice said to exude sanity in a world of depravity had turned a corner: we really should fear where the extremes of this age are leading us. Yet—fortunately for believers—sanity returns after prayer.

At the end of summer 2005, my wife and I spent our days in the district of Jihangir in Istanbul. While its views over the Bosphorus and the Golden Horn beyond were stunning, I was not too keen on those streets. In this secular quarter and haunt of expats, wine shops outnumbered grocery stores. These streets had a continental European feel to them and indeed conversations in French, German and English were often within earshot. Perhaps Jihangir's most famous resident is the writer, Orhan Pamuk, whose apartment I always passed on my way to the mosque. My heart in Istanbul lies in a place inland called Gunesli—it is not beautiful, it does not have grand views and its residents are far from rich—but in its huge mosque in its centre into which pour local shopkeepers for every prayer, there is a sense of piety. Jihangir is a place without spirit, a pale imitation of a Parisian street, losing itself in Efes Pilsen.

But on Fridays, a beacon lights on that hillside overlooking the Bosphorus and the Marmara Sea. The *adhan* calling me from Jihangir's eroding minarets, I would wander down the road to join my congregation. Nobody ever looked at me and stared, for in this land of different hues, nothing indicated that I was an Englishman passing through. Sitting on the carpet, the sun streaming through the open windows, the voices of foghorns down on the water below would greet us. Seeing young men entering in droves through the antique doors was a true delight, having recently returned from Artvin Province where the toothless, grey-haired ones dominated the mosques. These youthful faces were not locals, but came here for employment: my visits for prayer in the evening met with an elderly congregation numbering no more than five.

With every period of darkness, when my life seems so distant from the Prophetic ideal, I recall that beacon on the hillside. In the midst of despair there can still be light. And where did that beacon lead me? Warmed by *dhikr* after the Friday prayer, refreshed and renewed, we packed up and moved on to Gunesli, where *salams* are exchanged on its streets. Were it not for prayer, I would be lost.

Nationalism

I am not only a Muslim, but an Englishman as well. Ever since three underground trains and a bus were blown up in London in 2005, various commentators within the British media have begun to repeat the notion that multiculturalism has had its day. Political correctness is so year-before-last and racism is back in fashion. It seems that when a criminal act is perpetrated by people who happen to come from a certain ethnic background, we must always reignite old debates and engage in more philosophical acrobatics. Fortunately, when David Copeland initiated his nail-bombing campaign in London, killing three people and injuring 139 others, I was not forced to evaluate what it means to be a young white man in England these days.

'A year on from the London bombings,' reported BBC Online one day, 'the debate is firmly fixed on whether or not mutual tolerance has been pursued at the expense of something more practically designed to create unity—and the government is under pressure to answer tough questions.'

Newspaper columns and radio packages had placed a lot of emphasis on the government Department for Communities and Local Government's *Commission on Integration and Cohesion* that week. Rather, they had placed a lot of emphasis on problems within 'the Muslim community' as a result of this government piece of work. The terms of reference of this Commission seemed to be of little interest to journalists, who preferred to focus their attention on the country's only minority community.

What must it be like to be a Sikh or Hindu in Britain today? It is the Muslim community's fault of course: while many try to conflate religious identity with ethnicity—including a few too many Muslims—our diversity is turning us into a convenient catch-all category. To my list of minority communities I had intended to add West Indians, Jews, Poles, the Chinese and the Irish until I realised that I know a large number of Muslims from each of these groups.[61] Whenever I go to visit my friends in Hounslow, I realise that many Muslims and Sikhs are actually well integrated into their host community. It is just that adopting the mores and manners of working class English youth is not what the commentators have in mind. The United Kingdom— as its name suggests—has long been home to many nations and tribes. Yorkshiremen are famous for their regional pride. My eight-month stay in Stirling a few years ago gave me a taste of Scottish nationalism. London almost exists as a state within the state, the nation's media often condemned for being narrowly Londoncentric.

Had no one guessed by now, I am tired of these false debates. I am a multiculturalist myself, by which I mean I am multi-cultural. I am a Yorkshireman living in Buckinghamshire and what a potent mix that is. One of my grandparents is ethnically Irish, while I have an Armenian wife. My paternal grandfather was a strict Methodist, while both of my parents are Anglicans and I am a Muslim. My grandfather was of working class stock, working hard and making good, while my parents and siblings would be considered middle class. Define me as you will, but I could summarise thus: an English Muslim, quarter Irish, full-blood Yorkshire Cheshamite and Hamshen by marriage, and I am well integrated into multiple cultures.

Most definitions of Britishness are flawed from the outset. I was brought up in a middle class, church-going family and my culture was completely different from that of my best friend at school. Our country is naturally tribal—whether the tribe is being working class or coming from Yorkshire, or working in the fishing industry, or being a member of the armed forces, or speaking with an accent, or belonging to a particular Christian denomination, or being Jewish, or Hindu, or Irish. Multicul-turalism is not a policy: it is how and what we are. Did a massacre on our public transport system make multiculturalism a thing of the past? No. Nor was that the case when a small band of Irish republicans blew up a pub in Ealing Broadway a couple of days before my marriage in 2001—so that our Registry Office was decorated in blue and white Police ribbons on the day. Thankfully, many years ago the sane in our society recognised that there was something wrong with putting signs in shop windows that read, 'No Blacks, No Irish, No dogs.' I hope the commentators remember this before they push their maddening agenda any further.

In 2005 three underground trains and a bus were blown up by a criminal gang. What does that say about multiculturalism? Why should it say anything? Does it say something about state education? Does it say something about youth? Why associate the unassociated? If you have an agenda, construct your argument another way. The people who were slaughtered that day who are being used to push this agenda were of many nations and tribes, and their photographs say it all.

I am a native of these isles: my lineage on my father's side is English through and through. Growing up, long before I embraced Islam, it was patently clear that we have difficulties defining British culture. Just like any other, our society has always been split along multicultural lines—cultures of class, creed, political affiliation, dialect, region, social mobility, industry and so on. Because my paternal grandfather was a Methodist, he never drank alcohol, smoked or gambled. When he entered the army in the 1940s the Anglican chaplaincy looked down upon him as the follower of an inferior and erroneous creed. He often said he regretted not staying in the army, but my grandmother thought he might not have been happy in the long term. In the war years the other soldiers tolerated his abstention from mess culture—he would wander off on walks or go away to read as the card games, smoking and drinking commenced—but they may not have been as accommodating as the years passed by.

These diverse cultures of creed have long existed within British society. My good neighbours belong to a local church and their culture too has its own particular mores—they are lovely people, extremely kind, very generous, living a good life, attending church twice every Sunday and once every Wednesday night. This little country town of mine has three Baptist churches, three Anglican churches, a Roman Catholic church, a Methodist chapel, a United Reformed Church, a Free Church, a Spiritualist church, a Brethren Gospel hall, a Salvation Army Citadel and a Quaker Meeting House, all of which are members of a local *Churches Together* group. The faithful of each of those churches are marked out by the nuances of their particular culture. I was brought up as an Anglican in the Church of England. Unlike my late grandfather, my parents and siblings all drink alcohol, but our culture was still distinct from that of many of my peers. Beyond our disinterest in football or regularly going to the pub to drink—those musts of the monoculturalists—there were the social links maintained predominantly on the basis of affiliation to a common denomination, the home group study circles held in each others' homes, the regular attendance of church, Sunday school and the Christian youth group.

I was brought up in Hull in the north of England, which was traditionally a fishing economy and the culture of the town had its own flavour, dissimilar to that of the mill towns inland around Leeds and Bradford, and so people from Leeds used to look down on people from Hull, and vice versa. I think, too, of the strong cultural identities of members of the Conservative party, The Salvation Army and the Socialist Workers. The idea that there is such a thing as a unitary British identity is a myth at best and an outright lie at worst. It is being used today as a weapon against the Muslim community—which itself is not clearly defined—by social commentators with other agendas.

Those who are obsessed with viewing Muslims as the other should perhaps visit Old Amersham, a neighbouring town to mine. At the top of a wooded hill there is a memorial to the Protestant martyrs, the inscription of which honours six men and a woman who were burned to death at the stake nearby:

> They died for the principles of religious liberty, for the right to read and interpret the Holy Scriptures and to worship God according to their consciences as revealed through God's Holy Word.

I would remind them of *The Toleration Act* of 1689 and that that we are not living in those days when men and women were burned at the stake because they were different. My own town has a long history of religious non-conformity, ranging from followers of John Wycliffe's Lollards in the 16th century to the growth of the Baptist ministry in the 18th and 19th centuries. We are where we are today because the British gradually learnt to accept that ours is a diverse society. We are Anglicans, Baptists, Catholics, Methodists, Adventists, Witnesses, Muslims, Jews, Humanists, agnostics... and this list goes on and on. Muslims play an active role in British society—we are teachers, doctors, administrators, software developers, lawyers, factory workers, shop owners, street cleaners, social workers and students—but like the Methodists and the Protestants before us we consider our faith a precious gem.

The Muslim community is diverse and the way of life in one town may differ dramatically from that in another. I am opposed to blanket generalisations about Muslim people and yet I recognise that problems persist. The Friday prayer is meant to be a joyous event in the Muslim week, a gathering which we are all obliged to attend as one of our religious duties, but far too often I used to leave my local mosque feeling irritated. Ours is a diverse community: while the majority of Muslims in our town hail from Pakistan, we have a population deriving from several continents. There are West African, Malay, North African, English, Bengali, Turkish and Arab Muslim families living here. We are a diverse community, but all of us who do not understand classical Urdu, including a significant proportion of young people with Pakistani roots, are cut off from our faith week after week.

I believe that the imam is a good man—I have listened to the sound of his oration and it is clearly lyrical, inspiring those who understand him—and I know that the situation in our mosque is much better than in so many other places, but the language barrier troubles me nevertheless. One day I watched him as he smiled with amazement at the story he was telling about the

Prophet 🌸, his congregation repeating *subhanullah* over and over again. Those who could understand him were clearly inspired, smiling too and nodding their heads—but there were many of us looking bewildered because we seemed to be unworthy of benefiting from his sermon. It was just at that moment that my irritation peaked. Why did we have to put up with this week after week, I asked?

It is not that we have a large immigrant community that has only just arrived, for which excuses could easily be made. The first generation has been living in the town for more than 40 years—as one old man proudly told me when he mistook me for an East European upstart who had to be told his place. Personally I am quite a patient individual and one who believes that change will come: it is only a matter of time. I have moved to this community having experienced the ethnically-diverse, cosmopolitan mosques of London and have had the opportunity to witness the behaviour of Muslims from a wide variety of backgrounds: thus I am hardly going to be attracted by strange ideologies. But what of younger folk who have not seen the world? Could we not say they are easy prey for eloquent speakers—no, not even eloquent speakers: just people who simply speak their language? I think we could.

I do not call on people to abandon their rich lyrical heritage—a dear friend of mine often opined how English poetry paled beside Urdu verse, and I believe him having listened to our imam on numerous occasions now—only to recognise that the common language of the land in which we live is English. I understand that the first generation was keen for its children to learn their native tongue, for this was the language in which they had learnt their religion and in which they envisaged passing it on, in order that the meaning would not be lost in translation. Yet we live in a multicultural society and this works both ways. The town council and local health service provide translations of publications and interpreting services, recognising that our population is linguistically diverse, just as foreign states often translate road signs and official notices into English to aid their international visitors. It is time that all the leaders within the Muslim community recognised this too. Following several decades of racial tensions between communities, many within the British establishment realised that something had to change, that accommodations had to be made. The result has largely been good, whatever the current retractors may claim, and it would be nice if the leaders in our community learned something from this experience.[62]

Pride is not the word I would use to describe my relationship with my homeland—primarily because religion teaches us to be humble—but hatred is not the alternative. The British can be happy to know that we have a national health service which is free at the point of access, providing healthcare to all. We can commend the British for being generous to those in need: whenever there is a disaster anywhere in the world, we will dig deep and give to charitable causes. We can be enthusiastic about British tolerance which—although it has been eroded over recent years—has granted us freedoms unparalleled in many other parts of Europe. I agree that Britain is a contradictory place in which to live—just as the Muslim community is a contradictory space in which to move about—but I disagree with those who claim it is depraved.

I once read an article in which the English Muslim author did not seem to like the idea that Muslims should serve this nation of ours: our minds should always be on the lives of others elsewhere, while we ghettoise ourselves. I felt like inviting her to engage with the charities I was familiar with, to see the affect of our over-there mentality. Social depravation, ill-health, abuse and mental health problems in our own communities are left untackled, the response under-funded precisely because of this attitude which sees only overseas recipients as worthy causes. The author was scathing of a suggestion that Muslims should join the police force, noting the raid on 3,000 Muslim homes since 2001. In light of the growing culture of criminality amongst segments of our youth—the four drunk Pakistanis who kicked another to death in London's Leicester Square and the Somali gang that beat up a Pakistani imam in Hayes are sadly not queer aberrations—the idea that Muslims should join the police should have been considered commendable. Our role is one of being witnesses and contributors to society, not of being mere spectators. Thus Muslims, just as others, teach in our schools, nurse in our hospitals, care in fractured homes and police our communities. In his last sermon, the Prophet ﷺ taught his followers:

> Oh Mankind! Your Lord is One. Your father is one. All of you belong to Adam. Adam is created of soil. Truly, the most honourable person in the sight of your Lord is the most pious amongst you. There is no superiority for an Arab over a non-Arab, or for a non-Arab over an Arab, or for a red person over a white person. Likewise, there is no superiority of a white over a red person, except in piety.[63]

In the teachings of Islam, the nation, tribe or ethnic group to which one belongs has no bearing on our eventual success in the eyes of God. All that He asks of us is that we return to Him with a good heart, having treated others as we would like to be treated ourselves.

Relativism

We live in an age in which mainstream discourse represents a relativist worldview wherein there is no truth, only ideas and arguments; all beliefs are generally valid, although some are more valid than others. For people of faith this has major implications. A few years ago, one of the discussions of the Church of England's General Synod concerned Christian witness in a plural society. Writing in the *Church Times* at the time, David Banting noted that Muslims expect Christians to have convictions as clear as their own. He was right. While diversity of opinion is of course to be welcomed, the mean-dering, self-conscious spirit amongst many does not promote confidence in the process of dialogue. Representatives of the two faiths need to define clearly what it is that they believe, not wavering because they fear causing offence. Honesty must crown any efforts at dialogue and this means addressing issues even if they cause discomfort.

In my own case, as one who adopted a different path, it is impossible to ignore the fact that my belief in Islam causes friction within my family. Still, I continue to hold fast because I believe it to be the correct way to worship God. Most people who are sincere in their faith hold a position similar to this, whether they are Roman Catholic, Pentecostal, Buddhist, Baha'i or Jewish. I have been told that my family and friends continually pray that I may be guided back to the truth. They worry about me, fear that I have taken the wrong path and that, on the Day of Judgement, I will be amongst the losers. This situation is just one of the things which come with the territory of believing there to be a definitive truth and a reason for our existence. On both sides we believe that we have a hold of truth.

Yet our relationship does not end there. Indeed there need be no conflict between the idea of a faith's uniqueness and pluralism. We do not need to be totalitarian about our faith—whatever that may be—because we believe in its uniqueness; it is perfectly possible to live peaceably with people of other faith traditions whilst maintaining our own convictions. Periods of Islamic history attest to the fact that pluralism can coexist with a one-way faith, however much today's religious puritans and secular fundamentalists may wish to prove otherwise. A survey of all the counties touched by Islam will reveal the existence of local and diverse culture. Consider the mosques of China, India, Mali, Mexico or Turkey: each of the designs manifests something of an indigenous tradition. Consider the mastery of the Urdu poets, the literature of the Arabs or the growing body of modern self-expression in *blogistan* and cyberspace. Jewish writers have noted that many of their forefathers flourished as scholars under Muslim rule in Spain. Srebrenica was once a glowing example of coexistence in the midst of Europe. It is true to say that our history was not all light, but for every instance of shame we can find another about which we can be pleased.

Muslim tradition teaches that Islam was the religion of all of the prophets ﷺ. At the same time, it stresses that there is one path to God: that affirmed by all of them, that none should be worshipped except the one true God, the Creator of all things. The fact that I believe this does not negate my contribution to a pluralist society. We do not need to pretend that we cannot understand another person's point of view because we maintain firm beliefs. Muslims believe in God as the Creator of all things and therefore as the God worshipped by Jews and Christians. A Christian, however, might well argue that this is not the case in view of their Trinitarian theology; since Islam rejects the idea that anything in creation can also be the Creator, the demarcation is clear. We may hold completely different beliefs, but we are not incapable of understanding one another. The argument for the resurrection in the Christian worldview is that humans are irreparably corrupt and so our only salvation is through the blood of Christ. Islam, however, denies the concept of fallen humanity and original sin. Does this mean we cannot talk to one another?

I believe it is a mistake for Christians to renounce their faith—to deny previously established beliefs—simply because they are now encountering people of other faiths. Indeed, people of those faiths expect Christians to hold their ground; the real source of discomfort is not religious pluralism but effective secularism. It is the latter which demands that there is no absolute truth–except this one–not adherents to other religions.

Unfortunately, this alternative view of pluralism has become dominant today. Conviction is aligned with intolerance, while those who reject the relativist worldview are accused of promoting cultural ghettos. Since the massacres in London in 2005 we have heard much about the failure of multiculturalism from politicians, journalists and commentators alike. This is nothing new. Over the past 30 years there has been a growing body of theologians determined to frame religion in relativist terms. One argues that it is a form of idolatry for Christians to believe that Christianity alone is true. This suggests that they worship Christianity. It is true that a religion itself can become an object of worship, but that is not what believers are doing by insisting on its truth. For the majority of followers, the religion is merely the transport towards an end; they do not worship it, but use it to worship.

Yet again I insist that the concept of pluralism need not pose difficulties for our mere existence as believers of different faiths. The question is how it affects our ability to share our faith. To believe in a path as the one authentic way to worship God and yet withhold that from my loved ones is a form of hypocrisy. In life it is easier to hide—fearing to cause offence by saying that we believe this to be the way—than to invite others to believe in what we believe. Because the dominant argument of our age insists that there is no single truth and that while some views may be more valid than others, all beliefs are nevertheless legitimate, we can feel uncomfortable when it comes to sharing our beliefs with others. We avoid being a nuisance or causing resentment at all costs. Even as this dominates, however, with belief there is always an uncomfortable feeling inside: one day, when our meeting with our Lord finally comes, will my family and friends not hold me to account for failing to adequately explain this belief to them? The uncomfortable voice within says that though you fear their anger now, there is something worse along the line if you are silent. For believers of whatever faith, it is the central dilemma of our age.

Partiality

Considering the world as it is represented today, we would not know that a key teaching of Islam is to speak the truth even against ourselves and of Christianity to love your enemy as yourself. Instead we witness a culture in which individuals take sides, not on the basis of justice, but of a perceived sense of belonging. That the starting point of any dialogue should be a commitment to honesty is a statement of the obvious and yet it is a point that seems to have escaped many. An article which appeared in the *Church Times* during the Lambeth Conference in 1998 in which the author summarised a speech given by Bishop Josiah Idowu-Fearon of Kaduna diocese in northern Nigeria on dialogue between Muslims and Christians is illustrative. Reading the article at the time, my main objection was to the final paragraph which provided the only link to the headline:

> Lying in the interests of the faith is allowed by the Qur'an, Dr. Idowu-Fearon said. 'We are dealing with a religion that is adaptable.' Even with apparently moderate and friendly Muslims, 'we know underneath that, if anything happens, they can kill.'[64]

I find the first statement peculiar, for in a decade treading this path the sermons and study circles I have attended have consistently taught that Muslims must be truthful at all times. 'Speak the truth even if it be against yourself,' is a famous saying of the Prophet ﷺ.[65] Indeed he is reported to have said, 'It is great treachery that you tell your brother something which he accepts as truth from you, but you are lying.'[66] Exceptions—such as in the case of a Muslim being tortured in an effort to make him renounce his faith—are hardly the norm. What could be said of the final sentence, which would frighten any reader? It certainly does not encourage dialogue on the part of Christians for fear that they might accidentally cause offence. What was the context of the bishop's remarks, was he talking about something in particular or was this a general statement? If the bishop was an expert on Islam, he would certainly know that murder is considered one of the major sins. There is no licence for an individual Muslim to kill if 'anything happens'—where there is a war, only the state can authorise military engagement under Islamic Law and in this case soldiers are bound by strict rules of conduct.[67] Vigilantism will always have its own rules regardless of the creed of its participants.

Unfortunately dialogue is often stifled by our own perceptions of ourselves and the other. Long before Jack Straw, a Cabinet member, courted controversy with his remarks on the *nikab*—the face veil worn by some Muslim women—a national newspaper published an article in which a columnist wrote of her perception and dislike of it. Over the week that followed, the newspaper printed several letters of reply. One of them was a response to a Muslim's letter earlier in the week which claimed that women in *hijab* are judged merely on the basis of their intellect and personality, not according to their appearance: the purpose of the response was to allege that this is not born out in the real world.

Both points of view may be seen as exaggerations of reality in fact, for there are many Muslim women with PhDs in Muslim countries, many who are doctors, writers, teachers and politicians, including the famous Turkish MP who was stripped of her citizenship because she dared wear her headscarf in parliament—but there are also many other women who face very real discrimination. What was clear from both the article and many of the letters was that most of us are unwilling to put ourselves in the shoes of the other to appreciate an alternative point of view. It is sometimes as if our ego is king.

Before I became Muslim I did not have an issue or a problem with Muslim women wearing a headscarf, but I must be honest: it took me a long time to accommodate the concept of *nikab*, even after I became Muslim. No doubt this was a cultural concern based on assumptions more than any particular reasoning. I would never have denied a woman the right to wear the *nikab* if she so chose—in the same way that I would not demand that those men in flowing robes in Sub-Saharan Africa who also cover their faces abandon their dress—but I would be dishonest if I said that my view of it was magnanimous.

My somewhat ambiguous stance on the *nikab* was the view of one who became Muslim—someone who was sympathetic to Islam and who took up this path. Dialogue is often worthless because participants start from entrenched opinions, believing that to understand is to compromise one's beliefs. It is my view that we need to give more thought to how we communicate with one another and deal with the assumptions that arise. This applies to Muslims as well as others. Although my early encounters with some veiled women were far from positive, today—through professional relationships, charity work and friends—I know of many women who choose to wear *nikab*. Nowadays I am not opposed to the practice for those who choose to wear it, but it took me a long time to get to this point. I would not say dishonestly that this was always the case and so I cannot start pointing fingers at non-Muslims who continue to find it difficult. Indeed, I would apply the same principle in numerous areas given our failure to adequately explain our beliefs to others.

We have been given brains which enable us to think deeply about whatever we encounter in life and one of the great gifts that we have at our disposal is empathy. It is clearly not impossible for me as a Muslim to appreciate where others are coming from. Consider the feminist commentator who wrote the article about *nikab* in a national newspaper: typically Western feminists write not on the basis of their informed knowledge of the Muslim tradition, but in light of the heritage of their own culture. The veil or the headscarf reminds them of the words of the Apostle Paul, who is often identified as a misogynist by European feminists, and thus it is associated directly with his words instead of the teachings of Islam. In his first letter to the Corinthians, for example, Paul instructs his followers that 'every woman who prays or prophesies with her head uncovered dishonours her head'. These words are in turn related to other sayings of Paul concerning women.[68]

I have no doubt that this backdrop plays a major role in the perception of the *hijab* amongst educated feminists. While Islam has a strong tradition of female scholarship historically, feminists view church history as largely patriarchal, particularly in light of later theological debates concerning the woman's soul. Thus this very potent distrust of religion persists in the minds of many concerning the role of women: it is not prejudice against Islam *per se*, but more generally prejudice against religion. Rather than working ourselves into a dichotomy of us-versus-them, we need to be more intelligent in confronting such perceptions. It is not good enough for Muslims to constantly repeat the refrain that it is Islamophobia or anti-Semitism—we need to get to the root of the matter, to find out what is really behind such concerns. Is there anything we can do to help? Do we need to explain matters better? Do we know enough about the societies and communities we find ourselves amongst, about their histories and traditions? Do we know why people may react in a certain way or are we just making assumptions of our own? It is a task for all of us—Muslims and others alike.

Years ago a friend sent me an article by a young Muslim woman about her decision to wear *hijab*. It was like others I had read before: a defensive response to the perceptions of others. 'So next time you see me,' the author concluded, 'don't look at me sympathetically. I am not under duress or a male-worshipping female captive from those barbarous Arabic deserts. I've been liberated.'

I had often reflected on Muslim responses to others' perceptions of us; indeed, on our perception of their perception. I had no doubt that we often do encounter hostility, but I wished that we would not expect it. I recalled the day I became Muslim and the weeks after it. Although my testimony of faith came after a very personal journey over a long period of time, my decision was immediately broadcasted far and wide. At the time we were in the midst of our second year exams and so I put the strange behaviour of many of my friends down to exam stress. When the exams came to an end, the same people would still only smile, as if embarrassed, when I said hello, if they did not just turn their back on me and walk away. Relating to other people became very difficult: it was a time of paranoia. Looking back, I came to understand the reactions of two (unconnected) women to my behaviour when I was not a Muslim after they had taken to wearing *hijab*.

When I first went to university, there were really only two things that I knew about Islam: Muslims do not eat pork 'because pigs eat dirt' and Muslims only eat *halal* food. I did not have an opinion of Muslims—I did not think they were all terrorists or that they oppressed their women. When I went to university I found that there were Muslim women there who wore the headscarf. I cannot explain exactly why I reacted as I did, but whenever I saw such a person my eyes would hit the floor, averting from her face, on the belief that because she wore the scarf she wanted privacy. I encountered a tendency to become paranoid twice because of the way I behaved, the women in each case new to wearing the headscarf. On each occasion my refusal to look at the person was taken as meaning that I hated Muslims or that, at the very least, I had a great problem with them wearing *hijab*. I really thought neither; I just acted in the way that I assumed was expected of me.

Since then, I have been there, almost in their shoes and I know just what it is like. Visually little had changed about me, but words were enough: without me even telling anyone, the grapevine revealed that I had become a Muslim. Most of those acquaintances that had never been very close, but I had considered friends, dropped me in an instant. They would blank me when I said hello or looked at them, and I came to realise that they hated Muslims or that, at the very least, they had a problem with something that I believed. Later, others—even my closest friends—would drift away: they did not have a problem with me, they said, but then they cut off all our ties. Experiencing this, it is easy to start thinking that everyone thinks this way, but this is not the case.

I recall finding people on my course periodically ignoring me. I would think that this was because I was a Muslim now, but often there was a perfectly reasonable alternative explanation:

people get stressed, consumed in their own worries and study gets on top of them. There are also individuals who do not know exactly how to react around the Muslim and just want to show respect. There was a time when I felt that I should show respect to others only for my intentions to be misinterpreted and yet I found myself misinterpreting the behaviour of others when they responded to me in exactly the same manner.

In the years since then I have encountered all sorts of reactions to me and my beliefs. I have encountered fascination as well as disinterest, respect as well as hatred, curiosity as well as well as the boycott, sincerity as well as mockery. I have met people who have asked me question after question about Islam, searching on their own for truth. I have known people who do not even have an opinion on Islam; who are not even confident that they can pronounce the word Muslim. There comes a time when we realise that every person we meet should be treated as an individual: we should not make assumptions about anyone.

Representation

Who speaks for the Muslims? Well certainly not many of our journalists, but the Muslim Council of Britain, the Muslim Association of Britain or our imams? I do not have a clue. Who speaks for me? This is the question on the tongues of the chattering classes, but I do not think any of us ordinary folk—the represented—have the foggiest idea. I just find it strange that having lambasted Muslims for our alleged non-integration, we are now expected to have our own devolved polity, which must represent us to the government and tackle extremism. This is crazy and it is making me schizophrenic: this journey of the soul thrust aside by the modern anthropologists' desire to reduce our faith to a mere social ideology.

Those eleven consecutive oaths in the Qur'an concerning the soul[69] provide the foundation of everything I have learnt over several years treading this path and yet the perpetual public examination rips this away, replacing it with debates that are irrelevant to me. For, at the end of the day, it does not matter who represents me in the world. All Muslims know that what is important is how we represent ourselves before our Lord. On that awesome Day, when neither our forefathers nor our children will be able to help us, each of us will be personally accountable for our own actions.

Take us to your leader: I appreciate the sentiment, but this demand seems to ignore the nature of the community in this country, indeed of society as a whole. British society is entirely fragmentary and the Muslim community in this country no less so. Who speaks for the Muslims? It looks like we have been turned into the miners or car manufacturers, and the search is on for a union to spa with. Set aside any spiritual dimension to our lives, for we must now have our membership cards at the ready; welcome to the National Union of Muslim Believers.

The nature of the news media is that, in general, it reports only bad news; the exceptions may include sports, visits by statesmen, financial news and the like. We would not expect to see a report on the news detailing the wonderful weather that hit Albania today or the absence of war in Utah. As a result, our view of those subjects with which we are unfamiliar can easily appear skewed. In the case of Islam, we are unlikely to come across the very good work of organisations such as Muslim Aid or Islamic Relief in the daily reports of the news media, although there have been notable exceptions. Every day they provide emergency relief to the most desperate people on earth, re-gardless of creed or ethnicity; they contribute to social welfare programmes, undertake community development projects, assist in literacy programmes and work with orphans, but such in-formation is not the stuff of news reports. This is also true of Christian organisations, but general familiarity with Christianity allows us to fill in some of the gaps in reporting with ease.

One morning I turned the radio on to discover not only that several of the stories had a Muslim theme, but also that they verged on the ridiculous due to the standard of reportage. As I made my way to work there was a debate on the subject of Islamic extremism. The author of a book on immigration and multiculturalism was determined to debate what was meant by moderate Muslims—40 per cent of British Muslims believe in the *sharia*, he argued, without defining the term, and so the issue of extremism was a much bigger problem than generally acknowledged.[70] He did not want to discuss the question of how we tackle those who think it is a good idea to blow up innocents on the public transport system; he wanted to broaden the discussion out to cover anyone who believes that we should pray five times a day and thinks drinking alcohol is problematic. But how was that going to help anyone prevent people from engaging in acts of mass murder, I wondered; how does insisting that I am an extremist help the nation?

Another news item that morning concerned the United States' terrorist suspect Zacarias Moussaoui's past attendance of Brixton mosque in south London. Anyone who knew anything about Muslims of course would realise that—as people required to pray five times a day—we will attend the mosque wherever we find ourselves. Thus I have prayed in Brixton mosque (once) and in the famous Finsbury Park mosque too (twice). I have also attended the Muslim Welfare House mosque in Finsbury Park many times, and Central mosque, and East London mosque, and a tiny Bengali mosque behind Euston Station. I have prayed in the Muslim Heritage mosque in Westbourne Park, the Shia mosque in Maida Vale, the Sufi mosque in Cricklewood and the prayer room in the back of the Salafi bookshop there. I have attended the main mosque in West Ealing and the Pakistani mosque five minutes away. I have prayed in a Bengali mosque near King's Cross that used to be a pub and I have been to the Murabitun mosque in Norwich. I have attended an assortment of mosques in Peterborough and the former Methodist chapel mosque in Hull. I have been to Hounslow mosque, and two in Southall, and I once tried to find Acton mosque. I have attended York mosque and Stirling mosque, and Aylesbury mosque, and Chesham mosque, and one of Wycombe's mosques, and one in

Leicester, and the Turkish mosque there too. Then there was the Turkish mosque in Shoreditch and another one up near Dalston. I have also walked past the main mosque in Dodoma, Tanzania, while I have attended many different mosques in Istanbul and Artvin province, Turkey, not to mention my flying visits to Izmir, Izmit, Rize and Ankara, and Mecca and Medina in Arabia. I have even utilised the prayer room at London Heathrow Airport and Wycombe General Hospital. I am sure nobody would consider this newsworthy.

A third piece of news focused on how a Muslim prisoner awaiting extradition to the United States of America had led prayers while in detention for a short period in 2003. Again, I had to ask, what was so incredible about this? In the absence of an imam, any of us can lead a group of Muslims in prayer. When friends visit my house, I lead the prayer. If I visit some-one else's house, my host will lead. In university prayer rooms up and down the land, students are leading others in their daily acts of worship. What were these journalists thinking? Funny frock? Clerical collar? Evening song and matins? No, dear journalist, it really was not extraordinary at all.

I would be the first to admit that my knowledge of what goes on inside a synagogue or a gurdwara is limited to what I have read in books, but I have not set out to represent or recount tales about Jews or Sikhs. If I had, I would be duty bound to educate myself about their beliefs, histories, cultures and practices before proceeding any further. The code of practice enforced by the Press Complaints Commission makes clear that similar standards are required of journalists.

In 2005, BBC Radio 4 broadcast a programme entitled *A War Against Prejudice*, which focused on a Jewish organisation known as the Community Security Trust and its alleged role in exaggerating claims of anti-Semitism in British society. I must confess that I know very little about the subject, but it seemed apparent to me as an outsider—an English Muslim of Anglican stock—that the programme had been made with preconceived ideas in mind. Listening to this documentary it was impossible to ignore the feeling inside that the programme maker had begun with a conclusion and had proceeded to build his case around it.

When the journalist interviewed members of the Jewish community—and Inayat Bunglawala of the Muslim Council of Britain—who would lend support to his thesis, he used ostensibly leading questions. By contrast, when he interviewed Melanie Philips—whose frequent anti-Muslim views turned me away from listening to *The Moral Maze*—he probed her fear of anti-Semitism without the impartiality one would expect of a journalist. When Philips recounted her experience of a woman telling her that she 'hated the Jews, because of the way they treated the Palestinians', the journalist embarrassingly offered his own explanations for this—that her foe, whom he had never met, did not mean the Jews, but rather the Israelis.

It is not for me to argue whether the premise of the programme was correct or not; two rabbis and a Jewish sociologist lent some support to his case, if not entirely voluntarily. As a casual observer, my complaint centred upon a form of journalism that appeared off balance. Sadly, those of us unaffected by reporting such as this were most likely to turn a blind eye. Instead of standing up as witnesses to truth, each community has invested in its own interests, often to the exclusion of others.

Whether we like it or not, it is an undeniable fact that Christians and Christianity are often derided in the popular press, in comedy and in literature. More often than not these occurrences go unchallenged and unquestioned. When the attack is on Islam by contrast, argue some, the response is one of public outrage: 'They would never have got away with saying that about Muslims.'

This is not entirely true. Whenever there has been an outcry in recent times it has always come from segments of the Muslim community itself and not from society at large. Voices of agreement or support from outside this community are hardly overwhelming. Meanwhile there have been numerous occasions when Muslim organisations have united in protest at the portrayal of Jesus ﷺ in theatre and film. It is unfair to criticise Muslims for speaking up in their own perceived interests or in defence of what they consider sacred, while at the same time complaining that Christianity is being maligned. There is no reason why Christians should not stand up in their own defence; it would be naïve to expect others to take action on their behalf.

In any case, one has to question whether it is in fact true that people would be censured for uttering negative words about my faith. As an English Muslim I occupy a somewhat unique position as witness to the feelings of those around me. In the workplace my religious beliefs are generally unknown and so colleagues sometimes feel uninhibited in expressing views they might not articulate around a person who was perhaps more visibly Muslim. I thus know that people can indeed get away with deriding and criticising Islam and its followers in public, for most often others will turn a blind eye to it.

I once listened as a colleague lamented that Muslims would never change after the media reported the arrest of a group of young men on suspicion of involvement in a terrorist plot—although they were later released without charge, the running commentary amongst my colleagues continued: Islam was to blame for all the ills in the world. More recently a contractor peered over the shoulder of a colleague as she read of the killing of eight Israeli students at a Jewish religious college in Jerusalem on the internet and, after reading the headline out loud, sighed, 'Ah, the religion of peace strikes again.' I had grown used to comments of this nature emerging from his lips over the preceding days, but his sarcasm still prompted laughter from others in the room.

In public forums too, we witness slurs against Muslims and their religion for which we hear no words of condemnation. Nobody would deny that the world today is awash with bloodshed, presenting us with the twin heartbreaking challenge of terrorism and industrialised warfare. Terrorists claiming allegiance to Protestantism and Catholicism in the Northern Ireland conflict over the course of the past century, however, were not labelled Christian Terrorists, but it is considered legitimate to use the formulation, 'Islamic terrorism'. When the now defunct *Today* newspaper carried the headline, *In the name of Islam*, against a picture of the charred remains of a dead baby the day after the Oklahoma bombing, there was no public outcry, nor was there an apology when it emerged that the bomber was in fact a Christian—according to his own definition of himself.

Representation is always complex. January 2006 ended with the news that a tanker loaded with 10,000 tonnes of phosphoric acid had sunk off the French coast, threatening to leak 80 tonnes of fuel oil into the English Channel. It had all the makings of a major news story. As the British press focused on the House of Commons' vote over the controversial religious hatred bill, news that Danish firms were seeking an end to a boycott of their goods was receiving scant attention. By the end of the week everything had changed; the tanker was long forgotten and one story was dominating the headlines.

Collecting my wife from the train station on 2 February, having just turned off the *Six O'Clock News*, I was foaming all the way home about the way Muslims had to react so stupidly every time a red flag was waved in front of us. Just after I became Muslim another convert told me that the action we had taken was a bit like jumping on board a sinking ship. That day reminded me of his analogy. Disconnecting from the BBC and plugging into the internet provided some relief however; I suddenly noticed that amidst the commentary from the Muslims of cyberspace it was actually very hard to find people saying anything stupid after all. All I could see were the silent images in the online press.

A set of cartoons had been published four months earlier in Denmark, apparently to test the boundaries of freedom of expression, although perhaps the nation had already established these boundaries when its supreme court ruled that a supermarket chain had the right to sack a young Muslim woman for wearing a headscarf to work. On 20 October, 2005, the BBC reported that ambassadors of 10 Muslim countries had complained to the Danish prime minister about the newspaper's cartoons. The story then disappeared for three months only to reappear when *Arla Foods* announced it would have to make 100 redundancies after its sales in the Middle East fell to zero. In this bizarre twist to the usual sanctions regime, we almost saw Danish companies pleading for a food-for-oil programme after Peter Mandelson, the European Union trade commissioner, criticised the papers that re-ran the cartoons.[71]

Throughout the day on 2 February, 2006, I looked on at a media set on making this the main story of the day. When I returned to my car in the evening, the presenters on the evening news seemed to be continuing from where I had left them that morning. The package was introduced in sombre mood on the midday television news; we listened as the reporter told us that another clash of cultures, like that seen with *The Satanic Verses*, was 'developing fast'. Then, turning to the other camera with a smile, the presenter told us how to contribute to the debate online. While sales of Lurpak continued to plummet, a self-righteous media began to fight back, as if chanting death to those who have no respect for pointless provocation; only calls to boycott Middle Eastern goods would have quickly faded when it was realised that the only Middle Eastern goods available were oil and stale baklava.

Apparently there had been a massive wave of protest across the Middle East, although at that stage nobody had managed to capture the thronging crowds on camera. There could have been a world shortage of wide-angle lenses, for every photographer went for the up-close-and-personal look. Still, that would soon change once word got about. One of the protests involved a group of men pouring lighter fluid over a Danish flag that appeared to be made of tissue paper before setting it alight. I should think, were it not for its obligatory incineration, Danes would be touched by the affection with which the protesters had recreated their national flag; one protester had clearly spent hours on his neatly crayoned standard.

Elsewhere, men whose convictions were so strong that they

had to hide their faces beneath scarves briefly surrounded the European Union offices in Gaza and fired bullets into the air, gaining prime time airing on the television news. But rolling into a town just outside London, a camera crew filmed men walking out of a mosque looking scarily unperturbed. Even the non-Muslim asked for his opinion on the street seemed to be oblivious to the media frenzy all around him. Unprepared, he stuttered something about nothing and shrugged his shoulders.

Personally, I believe there are better ways to honour our blessed Prophet ﷺ than to violently demand that a non-Muslim newspaper observes Islamic principles of not depicting the messengers of God عليهم السلام. Islam has always prohibited this because it sought to prevent its followers from taking them as objects of worship in later years. A better way of honouring our Prophet ﷺ would have been by behaving as he would have: curbing our anger and observing patience for a start. He endured much worse abuse, insults and assaults at the hands of his enemies during his lifetime than anything printed in those newspapers, yet he always behaved munificently, forgiving those who had caused him harm. Yet by and large this was the attitude taken by those Muslims who had taken to representing themselves. Indeed there were no ritual bonfires of tubs of Lurpak in the car park at my mosque after Friday prayer that week, although I gather that a convicted drug dealer thought it would be a good idea to turn up in London dressed as a suicide bomber.

On the other hand, the media was making much of its demo-cratic right to cause offence in the civilised countries of Western Europe—albeit a right they refused to afford the Archbishop of Canterbury when he presented a fairly obscure lecture to a group of lawyers two years later. Unlike those ignorant, back-ward Muslims over there with their quaint ways and failure to appreciate satire, those that work in the media are enlightened souls interested only in exploring their boundaries. They seemed to have forgotten that a radio station in Copenhagen had to have its broadcasting licence taken away in August of the previous year after calling for the extermination of Muslims.

They seemed oblivious to the wider context of the story, up-
holding the sanctity of freedom of expression without acknowledging what had already been expressed, even if by an extreme
minority. Whilst exploring the boundaries of freedom of expression, Kaj Wilhelmsen told listeners to *Radio Holger*: 'There
are only two possible reactions if you want to stop this bomb
terrorism—either you expel all Muslims from Western Europe
so they cannot plant bombs, or you exterminate the fanatical
Muslims which would mean killing a substantial part of Muslim
immigrants.'[72]

As that year wore on, I began to notice a pattern in reporting
that confused me as one who had always defended the ob-
jectivity of the BBC. One afternoon I glanced at their News
Online website as I often used to do when the digital clock in
the corner of my screen reached midday, the rustle of packets
of crisps awaking me from my spreadsheet slumber. The main
item spanning two columns and in prominent text told the
whole nation that Muslims were angry once again. This was
news to me, but PopeBenedict XVI had apparently said something which had offended Muslims everywhere. Before my
blood started to boil about whatever it was that he had said,
however, something else was driving me around the bend. The
manner in which stories of Muslim anger were reported always
irritated me far more than the original words. When Roman
Catholics took to the streets of India to protest against the
screening of *The Da Vinci Code* in cinemas across the country,
news editors did not think it so important to highlight this
story, leaving it buried as a brief in the world news pages
instead.

To my mind, the complaints were hardly newsworthy. Pope
Benedict XVI is the head of the Roman Catholic Church and
a man who considers Roman Catholicism the only true
religion; previously he had said that the Church of England is
not a real church. Must I really bother myself with his words,
or his quotation of another's? Why is it, I asked myself, that
every time we are offended by something, journalists believe

that everyone should know; they never give this much attention to the Church of England's General Synod, except when they have spent the preceding week maligning its chair, of course. Still, our public service broadcaster insisted on putting it as the main headline on their website, along with the obligatory link to 'Your views'. The 200,000 person death toll in Darfur, the 50 corpses found on Baghdad streets the previous day and National Health Service hospital closures were all an aside.

I decided that I would watch this one. By the time I left work that evening, I predicted, it would be a major item on the evening news and, before we knew it, the anger would be getting widespread coverage, lasting for the next few days. Yet I also told myself that I would not be drawn into this affair, for I refused to have my agenda driven by people that I did not know. I did not expect things to change: soon enough we would see the rage on the streets, the burning flags and the trampled effigies, unless we had the good fortune to witness a military coup in China or a hurricane in Washington DC. For the believer, there are the words of the Messenger of God ﷺ who said, 'Forbearance is the best of traits' and 'Do not act on your anger'.[73]

Frenzied, irrational anger, of course, is not the sole preserve of Muslims. Jo Moore, former advisor to Stephen Byers, the transport, local government and regions secretary, was once made famous for suggesting that the terrorist attacks in the United States of America on 11 September, 2001, provided the department with a very good opportunity to 'get out anything we want to bury'. You do not have to be a conspiracy theorist to ask whether there is any correlation between domestic political turmoil and populist scaremongering. When it is a choice between getting angry about a piece of clothing worn by some women and the fate of the National Health Service, I know where my priorities lie, but by the end of 2006 I was clearly in the minority. Although one of the many consequences of the latest shake up of the service was the loss of huge numbers of staff and the drift of some of the most talented of them to private health providers, hundreds of thousands of words were spent arguing about the face veil worn by a few Muslim women in Britain. Answering questions about health service redundancies, the prime minister said that it would be a matter of a few hundred. That may have been the literalist answer, but in the trust for which I worked we were losing staff every day as they moved on, tired of the uncertainty and worried about paying their mortgage, affording their children's university fees and earning their pension: campaigners estimated a figure closer to 20,000. Across the country we were seeing hospital closures and yet the nation was in a spin about Jack Straw's comments on the veil. There was something telling about the anger of the nation that week.

More non-Muslim anger was on the cards when an individual —made famous by his intervention during a speech by John Reid, the home secretary, to an invited Muslim audience in east London—was interviewed by John Humphrys in the prominent 8.10am slot on BBC Radio 4's *Today* programme. As the interview went into overtime, I could not help wondering who he was. He clearly had good media connections for, on my return home that evening, I learned that he had also appeared on BBC Radio London and BBC Radio 2 during the course of the day. Here was a man who very few of us had ever heard of before getting his views across to a huge audience via three primetime interviews on a single day, prompting a flurry of complaints from listeners.

Our community has a rich tradition of verification which was established to preserve the teachings of our religion from adulteration. Early on we had rules on the transmission of knowledge, textual criticism, chronological authenticity, papyri evidence—and we have detailed biographies of narrators going back a millennium. To this day, traditional scholars continue to grant their students a licence to read, teach, copy and quote from books of knowledge only once it has been deemed that their understanding is sound and complete. In light of this heritage, I am sure that many were wondering who this spokesman was and how he made himself heard for several minutes on three separate radio stations in just one day. All we knew about him was that he was apparently a leading light in a group the media named the 'Saviour Sect'. The thought that occurred to me just then was where we would be if those known to us—and who have the authority to speak for a religion and a community of believers—could get airtime like that.

A friend once sent me a message in which he wrote that he now viewed all Muslims as terrorists with one goal, which is to kill non-Muslims. 'I know my view is being warped by the news media, critics, etc.' he wrote, 'so am trying to understand why.' Although I cannot claim to be fanatical in following it, I believe I get a fair exposure to the media and so it was difficult for me to comprehend how anyone could come to such a conclusion based upon this source. When Pakistan was hit by a massive earthquake at the start of Ramadan in 2004, a number of Muslim charities received very good publicity on the television news. On the other hand, much has been said about Muslims as victims of conflict and crisis worldwide. What is it, I asked, that blinds people to more balanced coverage?

Some years ago I would hear a hospital chaplain speaking of a lovely Muslim doctor who would come to pray in the chapel every day, only to mourn the terrible way Muslims behave barely two years later. What is it that skews a person's viewpoint despite their own experience? My grandmother once touched on this, telling me that, as a child, she was told never to trust Jews and Catholics, but when she finally met people of these two faiths she considered them some of the most wonderful people she had ever met. She told me this after meeting some of my friends at my wedding: they were lovely, she told me, despite what people say about Muslims.

I am conscious that there are Jews that consider the BBC anti-Semitic on the basis of its reporting from Palestine, black people who claim that it is racist, working-class Englishmen that describe it as anti-white and Muslims who label it Islamophobic. Although some people believe that the media is uniformly biased, we would be hard-pressed to show that this was clearly true and yet we have individuals who consider themselves profoundly affected by the reportage they encounter. I never found myself thinking that all Irish people or all Catholics were terrorists at the height of the IRA bombing campaigns, however. I find it impossible to comprehend that a person could be so heavily swayed by the news media; if it is a genuine occurrence, I can only conclude that my own viewpoint is affected by the conscious decisions that I have made, such as disposing of our television set.

A number of my friends have given up interfacing with the media altogether, recognising the addiction for what it is. It is unnatural, says one of them: only a century ago our predecessors would have known little more than what was happening across the county. Important news would get through eventually, but decisions were not required based upon the breaking news. It is not healthy to be bombarded with so much information day and night, he argued. Other friends go on media-free retreats and come back telling us how refreshed they feel. As for me, I find my television-free home a true sanctuary and an abode of peace.

Long before I knew anything about Islam I heard a relative exclaim, 'I can't believe how many black men are becoming Muslim in London, given the way they treat their women.' The statement was positing an assumption about Islam although it did not assert it directly. 'They' was meant to refer to Muslims and the suggestion was that if a man became a Muslim he must accordingly treat women in a way that is presumably poor. Yet we could ask whether Christians treat women better—if they do and we can really generalise—because of their Christianity or despite of it, given the origin of the modern women's liberation movement. The fact that British women now have basically the same rights as men, in theory at least, would never be attributed to Christianity. Is it fair to apply this kind of reasoning to Muslims and Islam? Muslims, as individuals and societies, have a history just like any other person or community.

Do Muslims treat women badly—if they do and we can really generalise—because of their Islam or despite it? In general, people are influenced by the behaviour of the society in which they live. Religion may teach a certain way of life, but individuals will not necessarily comply; indeed religion may prohibit certain behaviour, but people have the freewill to do as they please.

In 1870, British married women were granted the right to own property for the first time. This right was obtained not because of Christian teachings, but because of a social movement within the society of the time. That British Christian women have benefited as a result does not mean that it should be attributed to their religion. Similarly, Islam categorically prohibits forced marriage and yet it exists within some Muslim communities. Likewise, a large number of working-class men of immigrant stock have a dysfunctional family life not because they are Muslim, but because their employment in service industries requires them to work long unsociable hours. In truth, the teachings of any religion are usually something quite different from the practice of its adherents. Paul of Tarsus—from whom much of the Christian church's teachings derive—insisted that women must not ask questions in church, but we would be hard pressed to find people considering this acceptable today.

Islam is a religion which has something to say about the rights and roles of women in society. It would be wrong to engage in apologetics, arguing that what has been achieved for women in Britain over recent years is what Islam teaches. A true Muslim society is centred on seeking the pleasure of God and Islam sets out a way of life for its adherents, male and female. Nevertheless it is true that Muslim women were granted the right to own property more than 14 centuries ago, just as they were granted inheritance rights and recognised as independent intellectual beings:

> Indeed, the Muslim men and Muslim women, the believing men and believing women, the obedient men and obedient women, the truthful men and truthful

women, the patient men and patient women, the humble men and humble women, the charitable men and charitable women, the fasting men and fasting women, the men who guard their private parts and the women who do so, the men who remember God often and the women who do so—for them God has prepared forgiveness and a great reward.[74]

Representation is always complex. Sometimes it reflects reality, exposing the truth and relaying exactly what is happening. Sometimes it reflects a partial truth or almost truth. Many of the representations that we encounter each day are borne of convenience, ignorance or simply market forces, but there remains a place for deliberate misinformation. Not every news report is benign, designed to shift a few more copies of a newspaper from the newsstand. Following a bout of hysteria in the press one week concerning the loyalty of British Muslims towards their nation, one individual posted the following message on the website of a popular newspaper:

I am rather getting tired of the deafening silence of an immense majority of British Muslims when it comes to condemning terrorism.

He was not alone in expressing such sentiments, but I had to question his logic. British Muslims do not print newspapers that have a daily circulation close to eight million like *The Sun*, nor do we have access to the 9.8 million listeners that tune in to BBC Radio 1 each day, the 13 million that listen to Radio 2 or the 9.6 million that listen to Radio 4. Like every other normal citizen of this nation, we have no way of reaching the United Kingdom's 60 million residents. That is why I have never tired of the deafening silence of the immense majority of the British public on any number of issues, for I recognise that the immense majority only ever talk to members of their own family, friends and work colleagues.

I have always considered understatement a very English characteristic. If something seems *bloody* obvious we would not then go to the trouble of articulating it, but apparently this is not the case. Back in 2001 I thought that it went without saying that the terrorist attacks in the United States were unquestionably horrific, so I did not articulate this when I expressed my opposition to a new war. I should have said, 'These barbaric acts made me physically vomit, but I oppose the invasion of Afghanistan.' Instead I had to put up with my colleague sending me an email detailing the harrowing account of someone who had survived the collapse of the World Trade Centre, telling me, 'Perhaps this will help you understand.' It sometimes seems that we have to be constantly on guard as to how our words may be interpreted by others. Sometimes we cannot make a point without qualifying it with a statement so obvious that it makes us weep. Except, that is, when such a qualifier proves that we are uncaring and insincere oafs who say we care, but clearly do not: in the wrong-way-round sentence, this will be our downfall.

We are often expected to view complex issues as if they were straight-forward questions of yes and no or black and white. Years ago I listened as a friend was asked to account for the conflict in Israel and Palestine by a non-Muslim visitor to the mosque. 'It's difficult for us to pass comment,' he replied, 'for we do not know what is really happening, we are not living there and do not know what it is like to live under such conditions.' I am not sure that his response satisfied her, but it reassured me: we have grown used to easy answers from a media which has merged news and entertainment over the years. I was happy to hear somebody say that he did not know, that he did not have an answer to what was, in truth, an extremely complex question. More often than not, however, we are not given the luxury of erring or being indecisive: in the present age, we are forced to take sides as others group us into convenient categories.

In a debate broadcast on the Al Jazeera television channel, a sociologist celebrated in right-wing circles in the United States because of her critique of the Muslim world once spoke of a clash 'between civilisation and backwardness, between the civilised and the primitive, between barbarity and rationality.'[75] Picking up on an article about this debate, a friend once asked me to share my thoughts on this former Muslim's views. I did not find them particularly extraordinary, I replied, for clearly we are living in a world in which there are clashes of opposites. Although I am not a pacifist, I am opposed to many of the methods of modern warfare; thus I would describe the use of vacuum bombs, cluster bombs, cruise missiles, high-altitude bomber planes, chemical weapons and suicide bombs as acts of barbarity. The clash that I perceive is therefore not between civilisations—if they even exist—but between ways of thinking. The sociologist, however, viewed what is happening today as a clash between the culture of the West and the backwardness and ignorance of the Muslims. Of the Jews and the Christians she said: 'they are not the "People of the Book," they are people of many books. All the useful scientific books that you have today are theirs, the fruit of their tree and creative thinking.'

Her framing of the world as us and them is not a reflection of reality. According to this thesis Muslims have not produced anything since the great age of science several hundred years ago, but while the concept of the West is a convenient category it is not a reality. Is there such thing as the contribution of the West? What we actually have are the contributions of individuals and groups of individuals. Christians, Jews and atheists have all produced useful scientific works, but so have Muslims, Hindus and Buddhists.

One of Britain's leading neuroscientists is a Muslim. In my own circle of friends there is a Muslim who is designing algorithms to detect cancer tumours automatically through medical imaging, having completed his second PhD on artificial intelligence; there is another—the son of a well-known scholar of the Qur'an and *hadith*—working in genetics. The contribution of Muslims to contemporary science is in fact vast, but it is not recognised by those who foster the artificial construct of the West and Muslim world.

After providing feedback on my friend's article at the time, I asked why I was being asked to comment, for I noted that the transcript of the debate was already making its rounds on the internet by chainmail. Was it the latest attempt to provoke Muslims, I asked, to encourage us to react as some did to the *Jyllands Posten* cartoons? Were we meant to call for the woman's head, to scream and shout, march and burn down embassies? Were we supposed to act like animals so that the conservatives could say, 'Look at those irrational Moslems—they do not deserve freedom and respect. Let us wage war in their lands.' Perhaps I overreacted towards that friend of mine, but this is the nature of a large part of what we call representation today: it drives individuals to anger, sometimes without reason, and then all we have is regret. We have returned once more to that most beloved epistle of mine: 'What a vast amount of timber can be set ablaze by the tiniest spark!'

Ethnic Religion

Despite having adherents across every continent, in popular discourse Islam is often considered an ethnic religion alongside Hinduism, Buddhism, Sikhism, Judaism and others. In Britain it is often thought of as the religion of Pakistanis even as its roots in the Arabian Peninsula are acknowledged, with some Muslims contributing to this image themselves in the present age of nationalism. Islam, however, has always seen itself as a religion for the whole of humanity.

The first people to adopt Islam included an African, a Farsi and a number of Jews. Within decades of the death of the Prophet ﷺ, Islam had spread across North Africa up to Spain in the west and into China in the east. Muslims have existed in small numbers in the British Isles for centuries, although in time many of them emigrated and settled in North Africa, Turkey and other Muslim regions; in England they were typically known as Renegades. In 1641, for example, the Puritans published a pamphlet about a sect of Mahometans—as Muslims were known in Christian circles—warning: 'this sect is led along with a certaine foolish beliefe of Mahomet, which professed himselfe to be a Prophet.'[76] Muslims have existed in other parts of Europe for centuries and it is known that Islam entered some parts of what are now Russia and its satellites long before Christianity. Amongst my own friends I count numerous English, Irish, Italian, Jewish, Kenyan, Polish, Portugese, Spanish, West Indian and Native American Muslims, amongst many others.

As a result of my behaviour as a teenager, however, some of my relatives initially concluded that I had adopted Islam as an ethnic religion. While I had a healthy interest in the agricultural politics of Sub-Saharan Africa and in ideas of social justice, I also had some rather dubious habits such as playing reggae music unnaturally loudly in Caribbean company and dropping 'ethnic' names into conversations for no apparent reason: 'The ist in me,' as I wrote in a piece entitled *Seeking asylum from the past* in 1997, 'not with hate, but in stereotyping empathy.'[77] Thus although it would be reasonable to suggest—in the light of past behaviour—that I was attracted to Islam for a reason other than considering it truth, the reality was that I had moved away from those ill-considered ways long before I chanced upon this path. My sole criterion for taking Islam as my religion was considering it the proper way to worship my Creator.

Even so, it is impossible to escape the spectre of the ethnic religion as one encounters the perceptions of colleagues and neighbours. My adherence to Islam is often viewed as a lifestyle choice: I could be a hippy or a Buddhist instead and it would be the same thing. Religion in general is commonly derided in the workplace so that religious-minded folk are considered fools. Practising Christians are often ridiculed: the symbol of a fish on the back of a colleague's car is considered a sufficient reason to knock their contribution to the organisation. A Muslim's adherence to Islam, meanwhile, is usually tolerated in the spirit of cultural difference as long as it can be aligned with race or culture for, although Islam arises from the same region as Christianity, it is considered alien. The native that embraces the alien is considered a fellow of somewhat questionable nature: a follower of fashion at best. In an environment that frowns upon religion in general, the exotic is easily dismissed. Yet the issue of ethnicity drives deeper.

In 1996 when I went to study at the School of Oriental and African Studies—a college of the University of London—I watched as a fellow student went through what he thought was a radical transition in his beliefs. Given the nature of the college, many white students arrived with quite similar views: they were generally anti-racist, empathetic for the under-dog, left-wing or liberal in their views and greatly interested in the affairs of particular African or Asian nations. Although this kind of leaning does exist to quite a degree within wider British society, including sections of the media, it would be fair to say that a Eurocentric and white ethno-centric viewpoint still predominates on the street. Thus the views found amongst white students at the college could still have been considered quite radical.

Young people, however, often have a tendency to rebel against the dominant environment in which they find themselves, as I witnessed in the case of this particular student. Like me he was studying Development and had spent the previous year doing field research in southern Africa. When I first met him he had hugely Afrocentric views and was very keen on deliberately making friends with African students. As time went by, I noticed that these views were starting to shift quite significantly. It started with him playing devils-advocate with his 'ethnic' friends, moved on to a passionate defence of British colonial engagement in Africa and later derision of the alleged anti-white ethos in the college. He had become a true radical—except that these views were not radical at all. They were only radical within his context.

I sometimes recall this fellow when I am in gatherings made up mainly of white converts to Islam. Many of us were able to make a reasonably easy journey towards this faith precisely because we had a more internationalist perspective on life. Like those students at my college, we too had a generally anti-racist mindset, empathy for the under-dog and left-wing or liberal views. But as with that radical student, there seems to be an increasing trend for some gatherings of white Muslims to descend to the level of racist exchanges, often about Pakistani Muslims. There is contempt for their culture, derision of their ways and a level of general stereotyping about this group of people.

There is probably a good reason why I have experienced more of this since moving out of London. The capital is a very diverse city and the character of its mosques reflects this. In every part of the city we find mosques that are not the preserve of one particular ethnic group, but are cosmopolitan instead. They also tend to have good or decent provision for women. In many places outside the capital, however, this is not always the case. Mosques are often split along community lines and Islamic identity may be indistinguishable from ethnic identity. In my own town, although there exist a fairly large number of European, Arab and African Muslim families, the Pakistani community clearly dominates. The result can be a sense of exclusion at the mosque for anyone who does not speak Urdu or Punjabi, although change is slowly under way. No doubt it is this sense of exclusion which fuels the somewhat racist talk of some white Muslims.

I have another theory about this attitude though. A prominent characteristic of the call to faith over the past decade has been the separation of Islam from 'culture'. This has led to a sense of superiority developing amongst some converts—of whatever ethnic background—and amongst young people born into Muslim families: that we follow true Islam, not the cultural interpretations of those before us. This sense of self-importance is a real disease, which has seen old Bengali men who have prayed in the mosque five times a day without fail for 40 years castigated by young men as foolish ignorant folk. Given that many of these unsettling convert discussions revolve around the question of their (Pakistani) culture—as if we do not come to Islam with our own—I would say that an argument of Islam versus culture has a great impact.

It is fair to acknowledge that the experience of many converts, particularly those residing outside cosmopolitan settings, has been the racism of existing Muslim communities. I once felt that this was more likely to affect black converts, but more and more I have witnessed white Muslims complaining of discrimination too, whether real or imagined. The children of some English Muslim friends of ours have been put off Islam because when they were at school their Pakistani schoolmates told them that they could not be proper Muslims because they were white—one was told that she could not be Muslim because she had Christian hair. My general response to this kind of racism—be it the refusal to return the *salams* of the convert or simply the reluctance to make friends—is to hypothesise that this community probably experienced white racism in its early years and has therefore become quite insular in its outlook. The views of an English Muslim in my town suggests that there may be something in this, for he reports that when he became Muslim in the 1960s race relations were extremely poor. Whatever the cause, the result is the same: the sense of exclusion felt by those outside that group.

This is all very unfortunate, for it sometimes appears that our community is at risk of splitting along quite rigid lines. When there is talk of radicalisation in relation to the Muslim community it revolves around a polarisation towards militancy. Yet the form of radicalisation that I sometimes witness is the acceptance of racism, and it is a disease which needs tackling with equal urgency. If many are now resigned to the fact that we will experience racism at some point from within the Muslim community, others of us need to act to counteract this. For my part that means continuing to attend the mosque and not giving in to prejudice or indifference. It means saying that the experience of some of my convert friends is far from the totality of my experience. In truth, the majority of Muslims that I have encountered over the past decade—whether young or old—have been very warm and welcoming to this stranger passing through; my positive experiences far outnumber those disappointing moments. I think of my 96-year-old friend who always grins when he sees me: his smile drives away any sorrow.

Here I recall why I am a Muslim: our aim is to move beyond our obsession with ourselves, recognising our real goal. Although identity politics is becoming the order of the day in many parts of society, believers should be God-centred people. The aim of the Muslim is to achieve the pleasure of God. He has made us into nations and tribes that we may get to know one another: enough said.[78] After this we remember that this brotherhood of ours is one brotherhood.[79] Although I know that the atmosphere in my local mosque is not what I was used to in the cosmopolitan big city, that it took much longer for me to be accepted than in the mosques of the capital, I recall that—revolving around *tawhid*—my prayer, worship, life and death are for God, the Lord of all the worlds, who has no partner. In this we find our resting place, our home. When we recognise this, it becomes less important whether we are accepted by others: what matters is whether God accepts us and whether He accepts our deeds.

CHAPTER FIVE

Turning Back To God

A few years ago, a close friend and neighbour of mine flew off to begin a life in a new country. For him the growing hatred of Muslims expressed in our midst had reached its pinnacle and he decided that his future was not with Britain. I believed he was overreacting, but still I watched as he packed his bags and then I waved goodbye reluctantly. Not long before that, another friend—a history teacher by profession—announced his defeated observation amongst friends: 'Now I know how the Jews felt in the 1930s,' he said. There was a low mood amongst friends at the time; a kind of fear permeating our conversations.

The days of condemning terrorism—with which we could all agree—seemed distant memories; now the institutions and personalities dearest to Muslims were under attack. Voices of moderation were being labelled as voices of extremism, and so we all felt under threat. The reassurance once felt, that a clear distinction had been made between terrorists and the rest of us, had disappeared. The ever-narrowing definition of a moderate Muslim and ever-widening description of the extremist caused little less than despair. Suddenly all of us who practice our faith were extremists and thus a legitimate target for the wrath of right wing, left wing and liberal commentators alike. There was something telling in my friend's emigration to a hot, unfamiliar country.

Exhaustingly, Muslims are perpetually the focus of attention in television programmes and newspaper articles. The modern anthropologists subject us to a bizarre public examination, never tiring of their quest, proceeding as if there were no Sikhs, Hindus, Buddhists or Jews residing within these borders. How many more programmes must we see on women turning to Islam or women choosing *hijab*, and how many more series on the radicalisation of Muslim youth or documentaries quizzing the eccentric white convert? Whether positive or negative the attention is suffocating, and it is all a distraction, taking us away from the keys of our faith. Negotiating all the talk of conversion, *hijab*, the status of women, terrorism and the permissibility of this and that, we wonder what happened to the focus of our faith. All these philosophical acrobatics ignore the focal point of our lives. Distracted by politics and emotion, any mention of God appears some way down the list in the topics of our discourse.

The main principle of Islam is not that we should not eat pork, although some Muslims would give that impression. I once learnt only three things from some early Muslim acquaintances: Muslims do not eat pork, they only eat *halal* meat and they should not drink alcohol. No mention of God at all.

The Arabic word Islam means the submission or surrender of one's will to God. A person who does this is known as a Muslim. This is why Muslims believe that the religion of all the prophets was Islam—it is said that at least 240,000 were sent throughout human history—and that all of them were Muslims. The first principle of Islam is encapsulated in the Arabic phrase, '*La ilaha il-Allah*.' This is a testimony of faith which states that there is nothing worthy of worship except God. The two oppositions to this principle are that a person refuses to worship God at all and that a person worships others as well as God. The latter harks back to the first commandment, that 'The Lord your God is One God.' This is known as *tawhid* and it is a concept which affects all aspects of the Muslim's belief and worship.

A Muslim declares his or her faith by witnessing that none has the right to be worshipped except God and that Muhammad ﷺ is the Messenger of God. By these words, Muslims reject the worship of anything other than God. This means that they will not worship idols, rivers, rocks or a person. By these words they recognise that they have a direct relationship with God, the Creator of all things. The second half of the statement indicates belief in the Prophethood of Muhammad ﷺ. This belief means that one believes in and follows the guidance which he brought. The first part of this declaration of faith indicates, however, that if a person were to worship Muhammad ﷺ they would not be considered a Muslim. In the current climate it is worth reflecting on why we are really here. We must not lose heart or go off track; remember God and He will remember us.[80]

A few years ago as autumn turned to winter, I noticed that there was something wrong with me. I did not know what it was, but my emotions were heightened, I was on edge, easily upset and very inconsistent in my day to day dealings. My mood would swing between the strangest misery and confused folly. The misery revealed itself in the tears that welled up for no apparent reason from the tiniest seed. The folly in the quick humour which would rise rapidly and then die. I seemed to be dissatisfied with myself and my heart ached, feeling heavy in my chest.

Returning to England following a summer spent overseas, I quizzed myself about my unhappiness and decided that I could change it by engaging in one project or another. Each attempt lasted barely two weeks. There was a group writing initiative, to which I contributed five articles before hurriedly retracting four of them again, turning my back on the project because of the melancholy which kept overcoming me. It was all ups and downs, backwards and forwards, proposals and withdrawals. At work I wanted to be a writer, then a graphic designer, next an IT trainer, then a communications officer; and then, just as I was offered an interview for the latter, I was resigned once more to my role. Perhaps tomorrow would bring a better day, I concluded; perhaps it was not so bad.

Verily mankind is ungrateful. My first job after university was very comfortable. I earned a better salary then than I did for the next few years. It was located on a country estate outside

Maidenhead, in converted stables between a lovely walled garden and a grand mansion with manicured grounds. The chairman liked his fast cars but he was generous to us, keeping the fridge stocked up every week to provide his staff with a free lunch. For some reason, though, I was dissatisfied, despite a great wage for the simplest graphics work.

When the company downsized after the slump in the market following the attacks on the United States in September 2001 and I was out of a job, I started my own business wherein I would pass my days creating beautiful books—that most beloved pursuit of mine—but I became dissatisfied once more despite the eminent works that were passed my way. There had to be something better, I told myself, and so I moved onwards to new ground. I ended up as an office manager in a busy training department, a role that brought me numerous challenges and adventures. Yet again I became discontented and so the cycle restarted once more.

What was it that drove me over the edge again and again? Why was it that I was never satisfied with what I had? Was my situation not better than that of the poor soul who sets up his table on a bridge over the Bosporus every summer evening in Istanbul to sell ice-cold, bright-yellow lemonade to hot and tired commuters? Indeed, was my situation not better than those dry, scorching days I spent administering an internet café in the summer of 2003, with the fumes of traffic numbing my brain? Or the hours spent serving prickly Thai and unsophisticated Lebanese cuisine to 300 customers over lunchtime off Berkeley Square?

Perhaps it was pride: pride, which made me think that the job I was doing was never good enough; pride, which got in the way of an honest day's work, making it seem worthless and me worthless as a result. I thought I had been stumbling away from a path I knew when I was younger and more devoted to treating the lump of flesh beneath my ribs.

One of the first books I was given to read when I became Muslim in 1998 concerned the purification of the soul. When

I reflected on those uncomfortable symptoms as autumn turned to winter, I realised that it was time to return to that work and others like it, recognising what it was that was creating this unease. My soul had been neglected as the smog and noise of a violent and political world obscured the reality of faith. As this realisation dawned on me I sat alone one night and prayed.

Oh my Lord, put comfort back into my heart and do not let me die other than as one who has earned Your pleasure. Take away this heaviness and ache in my chest and replace it with lightness and appreciation of the sweetness of all of Your blessings. Oh my Lord, let me return to You with a good heart.

Some months later I put my eldest brother's name into *Google* one afternoon and clicked on search; information about him came up in the first listing out of 476,000 returns. He had been involved in a number of landmark cases in the High Court and Court of Appeal, and Chambers and Partners listed him as an up and coming individual. I then put in my sister's name: she also came up first out of 51,000, with eight further listings on the same page for her work on single-crystal X-ray crystallography. I immediately felt a pang of regret, looking in on myself. In the next instant I was wondering what studies I could undertake to get out of this rut—to be something beside my siblings. A moment later I realised that only pride lay behind this urge.

For months I had been lamenting my place in the world of work—I commonly described it as being stranded—but I had decided just to go with the flow, to go where my Lord took me, to submit to His plan instead of crying over mine. Applications and interviews aligned to my interests had yielded no results; the description of my current role had seemed to be what I was looking for, but its reality had proved far removed. Stranded there, at last I began to recognise that I had a station according to my efforts—and others had a station according to theirs. Latterly, I had found myself in the company of intellectuals and had started to consider myself one by association, but the reality was entirely different. That friends of mine are solicitors, teachers, academics and diplomats does not alter the fact that I am a simple worker whose eight-hour days pay the bills and little more. Over a number of months, the past that led me here had preoccupied me, but acknowledging mistakes cannot alter time.

There has always been a reason for every path I have taken, though often I could not comprehend it at the time. I try to pray *istikarah* at every juncture and move onwards accordingly. Friends ask me what I aspire to achieve in life: every time I just shrug my shoulders and mutter that I do not die other than as one who has earned his Creator's pleasure. A dear friend of mine, now a high-flying diplomat overseas, once gave me a telling off in the final weeks of my degree when he asked me what my intentions were. I informed him that I did not know and he promptly told me that this was not good enough, that we all had to aspire to something. What he would think of me today, I wondered, if he knew that my answer nine years later was still the same. I have dreams, of course, but all I can say with any certainty is that I want to honour God.

I only have these pangs of regret every now and then, when I realise how my siblings are doing and what my friends have achieved. But what lies behind this? I work to live, not vice versa. That simple job of mine paid the bills, puts food on the table. Does any man need any more? It is only pride that fosters these regrets of mine: the desire to be a great success, to be a match for my loved ones, to be known amongst the people, but that is not my station. Those who have reached great heights did so through hard work and perseverance, for we only reap what we sow.

Between my soul and God lie my heart and my deeds. The greatest obstacle that has stood in the way of my own spiritual progress over the past few years has been me. I have faced addictions, desires and distractions that taunt me, keeping me from realising any lofty goals. I once wrote to a friend with some thoughts that were pressing on me just then:

I fear I am regressing spiritually. I am torn between chasing after my religion and other matters, but more and more it is the other matters that dominate. I feel I really need help to get back on track because I cannot sustain anything on my own. I can bow down one evening in sincere repentance, only to slip again two days later. It is like I am falling.

There were times in the past when such realisation drove me to instant reform, but now I found myself with a kind of dispassionate resignation which troubled me, the lack of emotion worrying me. Emotion can drive change, creating energy and impetus. Instead I had this quiet realisation—I knew what I needed to do, but did not have the great drive. I had a problem, I told myself, and that was me.

Yet another truth dawned on me within a matter of days. The truth is that there is not going to be a starter whistle that tells us that now is the time to start putting our house in order: it is not going to work that way. We are going to have to realise that we need to take action and make a real effort. It is going to be hard, but it is the only way. Perseverance is the key: we have slipped much and we have a lot to do to get back on track.

The initial realisation came to me within just a few hours. It was not immediate, for there was another trip-up before I got there, but at last I took myself away and uttered the remembrance of God for two hours in my garden. I took my little purple pocket prayer book with me and repeated every supplication that seemed relevant to my state. With it came some ease and some resolve. I just need strength and perseverance now, I told myself, for I had been down this path before. There is not going to be some great fanfare—we just have to get going and try our best. It is up to us to make the effort, for nobody else is going to live our lives for us.

As one of those unfortunate souls that frequently makes mistakes and then repents, only to repeat them again over and over, I am often found reflecting on what Christians refer to as 'the addictive power of sin'. Faced with this phenomenon, I believe it is easy to appreciate how many Christians come to conclude that there is no escape from sin except through a dramatic external intervention; while I would argue that their solution is an illogical extreme, given that we only recognise sin in the light of what God has defined as good and bad, there is no escaping that sense of despair when we constantly replicate the same mistakes throughout the years of our lives. Muslims are, of course, reminded of the words of the Prophet ﷺ that had God created a community that would not err, He would have removed it and brought one that would err then ask for forgiveness, and He would certainly still forgive its people.[81] Indeed we are reminded of the famous *Hadith Qudsi* in which we are promised forgiveness, no matter what we have done, as long as we turn back to Him in repentance, and of other passages from the Qur'an:

> He said, 'And who despairs of his Lord's mercy except those who have gone astray?'[82]

> Say, 'O My servants who have transgressed against themselves, do not despair of God's mercy. Certainly God can forgive all sins, for it is He who is the Forgiving, the Merciful.[83]

We are aware of so many words which give us hope, and yet the sense of gloom is real, for recurring repentance for oft-repeated errors begins to feel hollow, shallow and half-hearted. It is true that I am not the worst of people, but my criteria for judging myself is not the standard set by the behaviour of others; my errors may well seem insignificant in a world of widespread bloodshed, but the Middle Way is not defined as the path between the shifting extremes of the day. We judge ourselves against a fixed standard. The earliest Christians would have been aware that all was not lost in the face of sin—even the parables recorded in the contemporary Gospel cannon make this clear—but today's discourse incessantly emphasises the need for a redeeming saviour.

When I look at my own response to the errors I make, I see ignorance at its heart. Ignorance feeds despair, for addiction is persuasive. If we convince ourselves that our addiction is incurable—as is the Christian's theological position, even though we find that many Christians are in fact people of high moral calibre who are clearly not subsumed in sin—a sense of hopelessness is really only a natural response. In my case, ignorance affects me in many, seemingly quite distinct ways, but which are, in fact, all interrelated. An ignorant response to our errors is tied to the ignorance that leads to them in the first place. Yet still we read in the Qur'an that none despairs of God's mercy except one who has gone astray; He encourages us to repent repeatedly.

I am carried back to my thoughts during a recent sojourn in a village in Artvin Province, Turkey. People in that forested valley not far from the border with Georgia generally lead happy, contented lives and are self-sufficient in many ways, but I was still struck by the hardship of much of their lives. I met widows on the sides of those valleys, and children who had lost their fathers, mothers who had lost their sons. I watched as old men busied themselves chopping logs for the stove and women collected hay for their animals, each preparing for the cold winter that would draw down on them in a few months' time.

I witnessed much more than this and I reflected on it in light of my own life and the way I live it. My life has always been characterised by remarkable ease—I have never experienced real hardship—and yet what can be said of the way I live it? I am lazy and often feeble, capable of telling myself that I am doing okay when I achieve nothing in weeks and weeks. What my experience in the Black Sea taught me—and this thought kept recurring throughout my stay—was that our Lord must have far higher expectations of us than I have ever acknowledged, that He requires a higher standard. The great hardship I witnessed convinced me that my laziness and feebleness in the face of so much ease could not possibly be acceptable to our Creator. Taking stock of my life, truthfulness—not humility— confesses that there is not a lot to be proud of. I may well deny that need for a redeeming saviour, but I remain tarnished by the legacy of that tradition, for instead of striving against my lower-self, my laziness, my weakness and my emotional addictions, I have allowed myself to succumb to them. Jesus ﷺ was sent to sinners not saints, Christians often remind us, but we recognise that this was one of the roles of our noble Prophet ﷺ too: the point is that they were sent to sinners so that they might reform themselves and become the best of people.

Muslims believe that the day God created our souls He took a solemn oath from us in which we promised that in exchange for freewill we would do His will on earth. A billion years or more may have passed since then, but the passage of time and forgetfulness has never been an excuse for abandoning our promises. I wish I could say that I was perfect, that I am a pious believer whose heart is clean and strong. Instead, looking in on myself, the words of a 19th-century Scottish preacher frequently return to my mind: 'To good and evil equal bent, And both a devil and a saint.' I wish I could say I was perfect, but instead the recurring realisation day and night, even if I do not act upon it, is that I must repent. I have so much for which I must and its time is drawing near.

> Repent and ask your Lord's forgiveness before you leave this world. Before the world occupies all your time, hurry to do deeds to save yourself.[84]

I have been here before, but that is life: those recurring cycles and phases. Now is the time. And yes I will repeat these words in the future, no doubt. But now is the time. And if I return, then now will be the time again. So we repent over and over, renewing our faith week after week, driving onwards towards the inevitable event. That day when our bodies will not breathe another breath and our souls will hang there waiting—still alive, but unable to put forth any more deeds. Perhaps we will hang there in our graves for another billion years as our bodies become dust, but a day will come. How did we honour that solemn oath of ours back millennia ago?

> Repent and ask your Lord's forgiveness before you leave this world. Before the world occupies all your time, hurry to do deeds to save yourself.

Now is the time, and tomorrow will be the time, and a month from now will be the time, for every moment is the present until it passes. *Tawbah*—turning back to God—means to return to correct action after error, asking for God's forgiveness and turning away from wrong actions. We know that God is the Compassionate, the Most Merciful, but it is only when we recognise that our turning to Him is in fact His turning to us that we begin to appreciate the height of His mercy. At the head of every chapter bar one of the Qur'an are the Arabic words, *Bismillahi ar-Rahmani ar-Rahim*—in the Name of God, the Compassionate, the Merciful. In its etymology, the word *rahim* is related to the word *raham*, which means 'womb', and so Muslims believe that God's mercy envelops and nurtures the whole of creation in the same way that the womb envelops and nurtures each of us before our birth.

We cannot travel this road alone, for we are dependent on our Lord in everything we do. As individuals and as communities we often lose sight of our direction, becoming obsessed with our own ideas and aspirations, which, although innocent or well-meant at first, can soon take us away from the realities of our existence. How often do we abandon our ideals, taking ourselves off in directions that oppose the beliefs that we hold dear? Our faith—whether we are Christian or Muslim—calls us to peace, justice, kindness, compassion, gentleness, generosity, honesty, modesty and humility, but often we find ourselves drafted in to support one side against another regardless of where the goodness lies.

I recognise that laziness is one of my chronic diseases, but as I said to a friend one night, most of the time I am just too lazy to do anything about it—and that laziness prevents me from tackling the other diseases of my heart. Yet in a world of Alcoholics Anonymous for slaves of the bottle and smoking cessation counselling for nicotine devotees, 'the addictive power of sin' seems to be a rather lame excuse for idleness. In time, we come to realise as individuals and societies that our only hope is to turn back to God and follow His way, for we are dependent on our Lord in everything that we do. However reluctant we may be, a time comes when we can no longer escape this reality.

Just as I was meeting my future wife for the first time, my manager at work was in the midst of preparations for his own marriage into an elite Bengali family and the strain was becoming apparent with every passing day. The mounting financial pressure looked set to become too much as the family's dowry expectations appeared to grow and grow. It was as if he was purchasing a mountain of gold for his bride to be. Not long afterwards it would be my turn: what would my beloved stipulate? Strings of pearls, diamonds and rubies, 500 bars of gold? None of these it turned out. All she begged of me was a promise, that I would take her for the *hajj*—the pilgrimage to Mecca that Muslims perform once in their lifetime. It was the only treasure that could please her, the only wealth that would satisfy.

Hajj is an obligatory act of worship for every able Muslim and so I knew that one day I would have to set out on this grand expedition. Yet I thought that it would be in later life, if not when old and grey then at least in the years approaching that age. I was not ready, I told myself, to go on that great adventure. Although I had no doubt that one day I would perform that pilgrimage I had to give the request some thought for it was my mountain of gold. My manager feared falling into debt; I feared that it was a promise I could not fulfil.

As each year passed us by, my wife's yearning to visit the Holy Mosque increased, but I avoided making concrete plans all the same. It was almost allegoric of my entire life in so many ways and certainly of my relationship with my faith: despite a pressing imminence and acceptance of a promise, this reluctance continued to accompany me. I was indeed conscious of my oath, but still I tried to convince myself that its fulfilment could be postponed for now. I had not made adequate provisions yet, I would say as each *hajj* season approached, but this excuse would not remain forever. As the fifth anniversary of our marriage drew near, I finally resolved to honour my word and set out to make apposite plans.

A year later I would stand on the Plain of Arafat amidst two million worshippers and raise my supplicating hands up in front of me. It was on Mount Arafat, perhaps 100 metres behind me, that our Prophet ﷺ delivered his Farewell Sermon in the final year of his life. Having left our tent just after dawn that day and walked to Arafat reciting traditional words—Here I am, O God, here I am, here I am, You have no partner, here I am, surely all praise, favour and authority belongs to You—we spent the day in prayer, shedding tears for our remiss over the preceding years. Although I stood amidst the multitudes I was alone: alone before my Creator, seeking His forgiveness, returning to Him.

Just days before, we had wondered if we would ever see that day—another metaphor of our lives—for it appeared that our group had succumbed to 21st-century banditry. Our visas had failed to materialise in the days before our flight not due to dawdling bureaucracy, but because our agent had not submitted our passports to the embassy. We lost our flight not because we did not have our visas in time, but because our agent had not booked our seats. We had no place to rest our heads, not because we had missed our flights and had thus lost our rooms in a hotel, but because our agent did nothing for us except take all of our money. Today's brigands come in many different guises. Some may claim to be *mujuhideen*, while others ascribe to themselves Islamic legitimacy unaware even to themselves that they are no more than petty criminals, but what of the businessmen who sell *hajj* packages to hundreds of eager pilgrims only to leave the worshippers high and dry? Four days after our intended departure, I made the following entry in my diary:

21 December 2006: It is our fourth day in Medina in the warming heat of Arabia according to our own grand master plan. Shortly we will depart for Mecca and the wondrous House. Planned months in advance and carefully financed—*ihram* sourced a month before departure, suitcases packed two weeks before—but though we plot and plan, Allah is always the best of planners. Here I sit in my own study, warming myself against the icy air beside the radiator, the fog outside covering the hill across the valley, the house across the street obscured by this hanging haze.

Our flight was last Sunday, but it left without us. Awaiting our visas, Tuesday was the next available flight, but still our visas failed to materialise. We planned, hopefully, for Wednesday, but even if it had all come through our plane would have been grounded by the heavy fog suffocating Heathrow airport. Now we plan for Friday, our visas secure we believe, but the meteorologists think the fog will hold for another day or so. Perhaps we will fly on Saturday. Perhaps not. Perhaps we will fly to Mecca direct and there will be no Medina for us this time. Perhaps not. We plot and plan, but Allah is the best of planners. And Allah is ever with the patient.

We had wondered if we would ever see that day, but now I was standing on the plain all alone, despite the masses all around me, estranged from my wife, my friends and my travelling companions until the sun began to set, my hands raised out before me. There on the sandy earth I recommitted myself to God, driving away my reluctance as best I could, even if it would take another year for a truth to sink in, that there will be no foghorn to inform us that now is the time to start putting our house in order. It is for me to make an effort and, persevering, take action. Thus I committed myself to turning back to God, to return to correct actions after so many errors, to beg for God's forgiveness and to finally turn away from wrong. Over the years I have repented repeatedly, but what is remorse worth without sincere resolve to change?

It was on Christmas morning that we arrived in Medina—that sanctuary of the early Muslims who fled persecution in Mecca—circling the city and sending our *salams* to the Prophet ﷺ as we glided above his mosque through the cloudless cobalt sky, its white minarets a centimetre apart as we descended. Although we were only able to stay there for two days before journeying onwards for the *hajj*, our visit was filled with immense bounties. I spent wonderful moments in the Prophet's ﷺ mosque, in the middle of the night, in the morning and in the afternoon. It is strange to find that our stay was so short, for my memories seem to fill a week. How grateful I am to one of my companions who pulled me from my slumber before the morning prayer on Boxing Day: wearied by my lack of sleep, I would have snoozed until the last *adhan* had he not reminded me where we were. Instead we hurried to the mosque to pray *tahajud* and contemplate on the magnificence of God's creation, setting in place a routine for the remainder of our stay on sacred soil.

Travelling onwards, I would discover that our expectations do not always mirror reality. En route to Mecca by bus, we found that the famous golden sand dunes depicted on the big screen in *The Message* were the product of artistic licence; we found a rock strewn, grey-brown volcanic landscape. After entering the state of *Ihram* our journey took all day, passing by with relative ease until our arrival at the outskirts of Mecca. I was taken by the generosity of the charities that provided packed lunches and bottles of water for every pilgrim passing through. That feeling of gratitude was to repeat throughout our *hajj* as we encountered the philanthropy of others over and over again, even as degrees of hardship tested us.

In days of old the tribulations faced by the pilgrim on his journey to Mecca included the assault of ravaging bandits determined to make quick profits by pillaging the winding desert caravans. In our own age, say some, the road to Mecca is easy, a comfortable voyage by jetliner to five-star accommodation—ease, considering that my Qur'an teacher's grandfather's grandfather journeyed an entire year from his home in Algeria to Mecca only a matter of decades before. Though as that may be for some, others of us unlucky enough to encounter the 21st-century bandits know that all of us are tested by degrees according to our intention and will. My own *hajj* was filled with great blessings, too many to enumerate: the kindness shown to us by others, the generosity of strangers, the beauty of our two days in Medina, the ease with which we completed many of our rites. I was truly humbled by the experience. Yet with every period of ease there was hardship, just as with every period of hardship there came relief. Thus the most frequently recurring thoughts were of those words of the Qur'an: 'Do the believers think they will say, "We Believe" and will not be tested?'[85]

Though we travelled as a group, we were all tried as individuals. I found great ease in much of my *hajj*, but others in our group found it deeply challenging. Walking our *hajj* made it for me, but was difficult for others. Our stay in the tents at Mina as orphans to another group was a beautiful experience for me—there I discovered one of my closest friends from England as well as folk from the two villages I lived in as a child—and yet it was an uncomfortable period of tension for others. Still, where there was difficulty, it was always possible to see good and if not good at least humour: at Arafat I asked God to aid me in controlling my tongue and the very same night I lost my voice, as the illness that accompanied me for the remainder of our stay struck me down.

If for some people the pilgrimage is nothing but a dramatic spectacle—a meaningless ritual to the utilitarian mind—for me it was filled with symbolism. It generated a multitude of similes for my own life, my faith and the position of the community of believers to which I belong. Our preparations for *hajj* exposed our powerlessness as we watched our best laid plans disintegrate before our eyes. Our final departure at half a day's notice after we had abandoned all hope of seeing *hajj* that year was proof that everything occurs by the will of God. The prayers on the plain were a great lesson in patience: exactly one year on, as millions more flooded into Arafat to crown their own *hajj*, I began a new job which pleased me, lifting me from my morass at last. The construction of a vast shopping mall just footsteps away from Islam's holiest mosque—one of the world's largest skyscrapers towering high above it—became a metaphor for both the ego that belittles tradition and the extreme materialism that pervades our community today. Yet the generosity of total strangers also reminded me that the hospitality that Muslims were once famed for remains strong within this community. On *hajj* I found myself often impressed when I had been pre-pared to be disappointed, humbled by the efforts of those who helped to make our pilgrimage what it was and grateful for having been invited to the House when I thought I was not ready. A year on, it was I who had that great yearning to return, the craving to see such days once more. As I walked amidst a sea of humanity one afternoon—two million men and women of every nation before and behind me for as far as the eye could see—there was no turning around to go the other way or to stop for rest. So it is with our lives: we are travelling towards an inevitable event. All we carry with us is our heart and our deeds.

CHAPTER SIX

Striving In God's Way

Just as I was properly entering full-time employment some years back, a dear relative pleaded with me not to punctuate by working days with the prayers at midday, mid-afternoon and sunset. My employers, she contended, would not look favourably upon one who set aside a few minutes away from his desk each day to cast his mind back beyond the heavens. Such behaviour could not possibly be good for me at this stage in my career when my whole future was at stake.

I did not wish to be dismissive, but the memory of a university student—the friend of a friend—from my period in Scotland was weighing on me. The young man, barely 20-years old, returned home from college one evening complaining of a headache; within two hours he had left this life having suffered a sudden brain seizure. Nobody saw it coming; nobody anticipated that such a thing could come to pass. My fear, I told my relative, was not being ready should my moment come. A few months earlier I met a friend who was slowly recovering after an accident in which a van had ploughed into him, throwing him from his bicycle and leaving him with horrific injuries. A few months later I learned that a woman who had completed her degree at the same time as me had been diagnosed with terminal cancer and was dying. This spectre of sudden illness and the unforeseen accident sharply reminded me that I did not know when my end would come. I cannot afford to wait until I am old and grey—because my whole future is at stake.

To pray five times a day is a matter of religious Law. After belief in God it is the most rewarding act of worship. The Prophet ﷺ taught his followers that the bond between them that separated them from the rest of mankind was prayer, and his companions said that they knew of nothing which if neglected would lead to disbelief except this. If I chose to abandon the prayers that fall within working hours for the sake of career development, what then would be left? To worship God is to obey Him.

The Muslim who sets out to study Islamic jurisprudence will spend weeks focusing on the times of prayer, on ritual purification, the particulars of the prayer itself and the specific prayers on Fridays, in *Ramadan*, when travelling, when asking for rain and so on. *Sharia*—the Islamic way—is taught in sequence, centring on the key elements first. Students learn of the aspects of belief—belief in God, the angels, the Prophets عليهم السلام and the revealed books—and then move on to cover purification, prayer, charity, fasting and pilgrimage. For some this is almost all they will learn, for these are the obligatory duties of every Muslim, but others will move on to study rulings concerning vows and oaths, matters of marriage and divorce, of business transactions, of inheritance and of wills and testaments. Those destined to become judges and scholars will inevitably move far beyond this, but those topics are of little concern to the ordinary man and woman.

Why, I asked, should any Christian be troubled by this? Their forefathers did not set the Law aside because of the inconvenience it caused them or for the reason of distaste, but purely as a consequence of their theology as in Paul's letter to the Galations: 'Now that no man is justified by the Law in the sight of God, is evident: for the righteous shall live by faith.'[86] The character around whom their beliefs revolve adhered to the Law himself: 'until heaven and earth pass away,' they believe he said, 'not the smallest letter or stroke shall pass from the Law until all is accomplished.'[87] Christians do not argue that the Law their saviour adhered to was erroneous, only that their faith in him supplanted it.

To worship God is the very purpose of life for the Muslim and Islam is the transport towards this end. *Tawhid*—the unity and sovereignty of God—is the key principle of Islam upon which every other matter is dependent:

> As the word in its literal sense signifies, it is a relationship with the Only One that excludes a similar relationship with anyone else. *Tawhid* is man's commitment to God, the focus of all his reverence and gratitude, the only source of value. What God desires of man becomes value for him, the end of human endeavour.[88]

The source of value for the Muslim who seeks to meet the objectives of *tawhid* is found in the Qur'an and the *sunna*. Both sources combine to make up the Law—the sum of legal provisions designed to realise the moral values and norms of an Islamic life.[89] Yet in wider society Islam is regarded as a structure that must be reformed—if not ignored—if the real betterment of people's lives is to be achieved. Render unto Caesar that which is Caesar's and unto God that which is God's are popular words, cited with increasing frequency as the debate on the role of religion intensifies, but who will accommodate those who say that that which is God's is more than private prayer?

It has become fashionable to view religion both as a source and manifestation of backwardness in human society. Barely does a day go by without a journalist or social commentator scrutinising the actions of religious folk in the modern world, their tone often mournful and curt. The reformation, the truth of evolution, the feminist revolution and the success of capitalism were all supposed to have pushed religion to the margins, replacing superstition with the supremacy of scientific rationalism. Secularists asserted that it is for man to create the structures by which he lives and dies, for him to define who he is and who he wants to be. Render unto Caesar that which is Caesar's, insist those who deride the rest of scripture. As a friend at work reminded me one morning—taking advantage of the late arrival of our colleagues—religion has no place in this enlightened era. Religion is the primary cause of underdevelopment and a hindrance to social progress; it is man alone that must reform and modernise society.

Why can't Muslims be more like Christians, ask the more nostalgic commentators who seek to counter the immoderation of some of their counterparts, promoting accommodation rather than dismissive contempt: why won't Muslims recognise that religion is a personal matter? Why don't Muslims recognise, as post-reformation Christians have, that truth is not derived from divine revelation, but is determined by what can be achieved by it? Belief is a personal affair to be tried and tested, for human reason is the ultimate authority, knowledge the mere product of his sense and perceptions. Islam, like Christianity before it, is in need of reform if Muslim societies are to advance, their citizens appropriating the enlightened mores of today's utopias. It was only a reformed Christianity, argued some of the 19th-century philosophers oblivious of the age to come, that created conditions fertile for economic development: Calvinist Protestantism considered hard work a form of worship, while its Lutheran equal saw the fulfilment of duty in worldly affairs as the highest form which the moral activity of the individual could assume. It was reformed Christianity, not the seizure of resources in colonised lands, that gave rise to economic development. If only the Muslims would realise this, they too would reap these fruit.

Why can't Muslims be more like Christians and recognise that religion is a personal matter to be confined to the home and place of worship? Religion is a warm feeling inside; beyond that, it is the source of injustice and oppression in the world. Indeed, religion is a symptom of oppression: 'Man makes religion,' stipulates irreligious criticism, 'religion does not make man'.[90] Religion is but a reflex of the real world:

> Religion is the sigh of the oppressed creature, the heart
> of a heartless world, just as it is the spirit of spiritless

conditions. It is the opium of the people. ... To abolish religion as the illusory happiness of the people is to demand their real happiness.[91]

The contemporary preoccupation with viewing religion as a cause and symptom of backwardness is in fact nothing new. Some of yesterday's atheists went beyond mockery—'science has liberated us from believing in sky pixies'—and built societies in which religion really did have no place. Lenin held that religion was a form of spiritual oppression, a mechanism which weighed down heavily on the majority of people: rather than motivating people to better their lives, it taught the exploited classes to await the next world passively, taking comfort in the hope of heavenly reward.[92] Thus the early years of the 20th century saw religion ridiculed by the League of the Militant Godless in the Soviet Union, while atheism was promulgated through education and the media. Although Albania under Enver Hoxha was alone in actually banning religion, other countries played an active role in persecuting religious leaders, institutions and the ordinary believer.

It is true that the most vulnerable members of society are often the first to make up religious followings, but far from it being a defeated sigh, the phenomenon can be seen as a manifestation of empowerment. In Rwanda in east Africa, the number of Muslims has doubled since the genocide of 1994 and now they make up 14 per cent of the population. A large number of them say they adopted Islam after witnessing the role played in the massacres by some Catholic and Protestant leaders. While thousands were slaughtered even as they sought refuge beneath church roofs, Muslim families and the leaders of their communities hid and guarded many of those who could escape:

'If it weren't for the Muslims, my whole family would be dead,' said Aisha Uwimbabazi, 27, a convert and mother of two children. 'I was very, very thankful for Muslim people during the genocide...'[93]

Similarly it is thought that their growing awareness of social degradation motivated thousands of untouchable caste Harijan Hindus in several villages in Tinnevelly district of Tamil Nadu in India to embrace Islam years earlier.[94] For many, religion is a theology of liberation, but reservations about its role in society remain. While mainstream Christianity considers relief work a crucial constituent of true faith, one author proves that some interpretations are less than positive, as in his description of the phenomenon of Dispensationalist theology which actively encourages its adherents to believe that they should submit to adversity passively:

> In 1989 I heard a pastor in Greenville, Liberia, preach on Revelation 6, 1-8, a passage which deals with four horsemen given authority over a quarter of the earth 'to kill by the sword, by famine, by plague and by wild beasts'. He claimed that this text was being fulfilled at that very time. He linked the prophecy of famine with Liberia's food shortages ... Rice was said to be scarce because it was God's plan; since it was God's plan, nothing could be done about it... The Christian's role in these circumstances was merely to trust in Jesus...[95]

The role of religion in society is far more complex than many of us wish to acknowledge. We cannot generalise about the irreligious—my friend who designs particle accelerators for a living has beliefs entirely distinct from those of my old Marxist flatmate—but it is apparently acceptable to simplify the interactions of creed and community. The demand that Islam be reformed because that was the path taken by western Christianity supposes an experience of history that is universal. We must suppress religion, argue some of its detractors, for religion suppressed the pursuit of science. Indeed an industry has developed over recent years whose very aim is to write-off the beliefs of religious folk, placing science in one camp and religion in the other. Yet, in truth, it was only a particular strand of Christianity during a particular period of its history that proved resistant to scientific exploration. The contribution of Muslim scholars to the fields of economy, engineering, geography, mathematics, medicine and science over several hundred years whilst Europe lingered in its Dark Ages is well documented. There was consensus amongst Muslim scholars nine centuries ago, for example, that the Earth is round like an ostrich egg, not flat like a pancake. The hospitals of the medieval Muslim world, meanwhile, were renowned for their advances in healthcare. That the Muslim physician Ibn Al-Nafis explained the basic principles of pulmonary circulation nearly 350 years before the birth of Sir William Harvey, who is credited with first proposing the theory in Europe, is but one of hundreds of examples of systematic exploration in the pre-enlightenment age. Islam itself teaches that the acquisition of knowledge is obligatory for all Muslim men and women.

Where does this leave us? In exactly the same position, apparently. Though the Muslim argues that the current social morass is the natural consequence of the neglect of Islam's teachings—over the past two centuries Muslims have experimented with nationalism and socialism in its place—a different paradigm prevails. Sociologists charge Islam with being the source of discrimination against women. Strategists blame it for the rise of militancy. Secular economists insist that it is a negative influence on the development of society. It is the antithesis of progressiveness, they claim, and thus irrelevant to industrial civilisation.

I beg to differ, for care for one's neighbour lies at the heart of a God-centred society. Although policy-makers place emphasis on social well-being and the needs of the poor in general, it remains the case that economic growth is widely held to be society's primary concern. A nation that views economic growth as an end in itself may fail to satisfy the deeper needs of its people, but the failure to achieve growth may have the same consequences. In the absence of great wealth, development is dependent on growth:

Clearly, if a whole population is desperately poor, growth is the only way any of them (let alone all) will ever be able to have their plight eased. If only a part of the population is desperately poor, growth permits the suffering of the poor to be alleviated without penalising the non-poor as much as would have been the case without growth.[96]

Long-term growth is the aim of all major economies, whether it is an end in itself or, as is more likely, the means of securing public welfare. Rich economies concentrate on controlling resources in order to achieve optimum productivity, manipulating interest rates to control capital funds and to decrease borrowing expenditure, so as to allow the government to guide the economy to meet its current needs. At times of high unemployment, monetary policy may aim to develop economic activity in order to lower its rate. Under the Keynesian model it is said that increased capital supply contributes to lowering interest rates; where interest rates rise, the incentive to save increases, while incentive to invest decreases. Increased investment causes a rise in demand, which in turn should lead to increased economic activity.[97]

The Qur'an is not a treatise of political economy but it has been noted that more than 1,400 of its 6,226 verses refer to economic issues. On economic growth, one author has noted that several verses encourage the exploitation of resources so that poverty is minimised, while income and wealth increases, although the accumulation of wealth is tied to particular conditions.[98] Wealth is permissible only when it is obtained through legal means defined by Islamic Law; wealth acquired through gambling, the sale of alcohol or illegal drugs or from interest, for example, is considered *haram*.

Long before the Make Poverty History campaign caught the public imagination—its huge momentum so famously derailed by four bombs on the London transport system in July 2005—another global movement was calling for the cancellation of the unpayable debts of the world's poorest countries. At the turn of the millennium, Africa was said to be paying $200 million every week just to service its debts. 'The debts are unjust, unpayable and are killing too many people,' lamented Jubilee 2000, 'The cards are stacked against the poor. We've got to change the system, to put an end to this injustice.' Thus, in more than 120 countries, trade unions, charities, religious groups and community organisations came together with a unified retort; a call that the debt be dropped.

There is no doubt that this was a noble cause. It is claimed that Benin used more than 50 per cent of the money saved through debt relief to fund healthcare, while Tanzania was able to abolish primary school fees which led to an increase in attendance of more than 60 per cent. The work of Jubilee 2000 was indeed commendable. Yet for those of us familiar with religious law it does seem that we are missing something. While calling for the cancellation of existing debts, there is a much larger injustice about which we have fallen silent.

For several years, low income countries paid about $2.30 to service their debts for every $1 received in grant aid. In her well-known book, *A Fate Worse Than Debt*, Susan George called interest rates the 'bane of Third World debtors' existence'.[99] Interest lies at the heart of the matter. The first loans to Africa, Asia and South America came from the World Bank and foreign governments, targeted at development projects and the expansion of capital goods imports and were tied to relatively low interest rates. It is ironic that the newly oil-rich Muslim countries of the Middle East should be responsible, even if in-directly, for the crisis of later years.

In the 1970s, commercial banks inexperienced in dealing with poor countries found themselves holding excess capital from Opec's oil price partnership and thus provided variable-rate loans based on market rates. Interest rates followed market fluctuations and, largely as a result of the US Federal Reserve tightening monetary policy against inflation in the 1980s, they quickly rose from negative to positive levels. Consequently, as debt repayments suffered, the commercial banks withdrew from further lending to protect their own interests. The result of continued high interest rates, combined with a decline in commercial bank lending, was the paradox that the recipient countries were paying out more finance servicing payments than they received as borrowing.

Although some progress has already been made towards re-alising its goal, the Jubilee Debt Campaign, as it is now known, is demanding a complete end to the injustice of what has been termed the 'Third World debt crisis'. Admirable, indeed, but is it not time that we addressed the issue at the heart of this crisis? The movement's name derives from the Hebrew Bible, for the jubilee was a time when debts would be forgiven. In *The Times* in 1998, the late Roman Catholic Archbishop Cardinal Hume wrote: 'The prospect of reducing the burden of debt has profound theological resonance.'[100] A step further could have equally heartfelt significance, for in this crisis there is an inkling of a matter that was always treated with due concern by Church theologians through the ages.

Judaism, Christianity and Islam have much in common, one example of which is a prohibition on the consumption or charge of interest. Traditionally all three faiths held that contracting a transaction involving interest was a major sin. The Law in the Pentateuch states that an Israelite may not exact interest from his poor brother on a loan given to him. A Jewish court would reject a contract based on usury made between Jews. In the Psalms it is written that one who does not put his money out to usury will remain unshaken. In Ezekiel, a righteous man is one who 'never lends either at discount or at interest, but shuns injustice and deals fairly between one person and another'; a loan in interest, meanwhile, is considered amongst a list of abominations.[101]

Similarly, Christians made reference to the Gospel of Luke which advises believers to lend without expecting a return. The *Encyclical* of Pope Benedict XIV of 1745 stated, 'The nature of the sin called usury has its proper place and origin in a loan contract.' He went on, 'One cannot condone the sin of usury by arguing that the gain is not great or excessive, but rather moderate or small; neither can it be condoned by arguing that the borrower is rich; nor even by arguing that the money borrowed is not left idle, but is spent usefully...'[102]

As for Muslims, the Qur'an states, 'Those who devour usury will not stand except as stand one whom the devil by his touch has driven to madness. That is because they say: trade is like usury, but God has permitted trade and forbidden usury...'[103] The prohibition of interest—*riba* in Arabic—is mentioned in five verses of the Qur'an and condemned several times within the *sunna*. Our blessed Prophet ﷺ confirmed this when he said, 'A dirham which a man knowingly receives in usury is more serious a sin than 36 acts of adultery.'[104] Some authors have argued that this prohibition does not refer to interest in general, but refers to the pre-Islamic practice of doubling an overdue debt.[105] This argument, however, is divergent from the consensus of Islamic opinion: it is akin to stating that only some alcoholic drinks are prohibited because the Qur'an uses the word *khamr* which refers to a specific kind of drink made from grapes. Islamic jurists are agreed that *riba* refers to an excess of money demanded over the principal sum loaned for a specified period of time in financial transactions.

It should not be difficult to appreciate how a disassociation from interest would have the greatest theological resonance, but we actually find that most people are ignorant of this tradition. Although a distinction between usury and interest was rejected by both Luther and Phillip Melanchthon, Calvin's separation of the two gradually gained acceptance amongst both Protestants and Catholics. Thus, today, in a global economy based on interest, few give the matter a second thought. Indeed this is surely the age that the Prophet ﷺ spoke of when he said, 'A time is certainly coming to mankind when only the receiver of usury will remain and if he does not receive it, some of its smoke will reach him.'[106] It is time that we stopped skirting around the issue. It is not just the debts which are unjust, unpayable and which are killing too many people, as the Drop the Debt campaign argued. It has been noted that income generated by interest is seen to create a rentier class that becomes a burden on the progress of society as a whole and leads to waste in productive potential. In simple terms, it is viewed as being unjust; because it is the poor who are usually debtors, the likelihood of them gaining from interest is extremely low. All of us would do well to support this admirable and worthwhile campaign, but we should recognise that it is only part of the solution. If we—believers of the Abrahamic faiths—really want to change the system, we may have to concede that it is time to stick Calvin's separation back together again and that maybe—just maybe—the ancients had it right after all.

'And so you would have us live in a primitive society,' retorts the economist.

'I would have us live in a fairer society,' I might reply, for I recognise that the way we live comes at a price. When I speak of my concern about the cost of our wants, I do not do so as an untainted Luddite living a lifestyle untouched by modernity–I own a computer, a washing machine, a mobile phone and various other gadgets—but rather as an uncomfortable technophile. Consider the life cycle of tantalum alone, which is used to manufacture capacitors which maintain the flow of current in electronic devices. This valuable commodity is refined from colombo-tantalite, also known as coltan, which is mined in countries such as the Democratic Republic of Congo which holds 80 per cent of the world's deposits.

In the mid-1990s, Ugandan and Rwandan armed forces moved into the Congolese regions that have the highest mining yields, took control of them and continue to maintain a monopoly there, making them in excess of $20 million a month during a period of bloody war involving nine African nations and directly affecting the lives of 50 million people. Between August 1998 and April 2004, when most of the fighting occurred, it is estimated that 3.8 million people died. Despite vast mineral exports it is one of the most impoverished nations on earth.

Our desire for the latest gadget—even when it does not add any value over the models it replaces—is fuelling this conflict, even if we hate to acknowledge it. It has been said that the highest-selling mobile phone with touch screen controls and exquisite branding, contains three times the quantity of tantalum than the handsets of its competitors; even if this tantalum was mined in Colombia, the demand for coltan naturally maintains the mining frenzy in Congo.

In Britain a political economy has developed in which many of us have convinced ourselves that we must always have something new—the latest mobile phone, better furniture, new clothes—and a culture of credit has been promoted to support it. Several times a month I receive letters from credit card and personal loan companies, suggesting that I might buy myself a new car or go on an exotic holiday if I signed up to take advantage of their attractive product. We are sold on the perpetual upgrade, although we are well aware that resources are finite, and we demand an economy that will always sustain much more than our needs.

There is an alternative, for history proves that wealthy societies have existed in the absence of economies based on interest, given autonomous control of resources. On the small scale an institution known as *'udha* sale was used as a substitute for interest in the Hadramawy region of Yemen in the 19th century. Based on the revocable sale of the custody of property, this allowed Muslims to take credit without violating the prohibition.[107] In contemporary literature on Islamic economics the main alternative to the use of interest is the principle of profit and loss sharing, the most important of which is known as *mudaraba*. This is a long-term precautionary saving facility which gives depositors a share of the bank's profits; in circumstances of loss the depositors do not win a profit share, but their deposit is guaranteed against liquidation. Profit and loss sharing is a useful economic framework that has been practised for thousands of years: 'In many markets and for various types of lenders, borrowers, savers, and investors,' wrote one economist, 'profit and loss sharing is the preferred mechanism for allocating returns even when interest is a legally available option.'[108]

Yet as Pope Paul VI pointed out in his *Populorum Progressio,* development cannot be confined to economic growth alone: it should promote human welfare and spiritual growth.[109] While there are many approaches to the definition of human welfare, a common strand focuses on basic needs which address the absolutely poor. Recognising the failure of economic growth to alleviate poverty in developing countries many development economists adopted a basic needs approach beginning in the 1970s with the aim of ensuring that everyone has access to enough basic goods and services to maintain a level of living above a basic minimum.[110] The sum of individual utilities is usually taken as the measure of social welfare and a measure of poverty is often lowness of income. The World Bank defines poverty as the inability of an individual to attain a minimum standard of living, but it has been argued that it makes more sense to view poverty as capability deprivation, taking the free-dom an individual has to avoid hunger or homelessness into account.

Although the family is considered the basic social unit within the framework of Islam, its role is rarely studied in contemporary literature on Islamic economics. Traditionally it only became the responsibility of an Islamic government to meet the needs of its subjects when the family and the community were unable do so, although structures of social welfare were well established in the medieval Muslim world.[111] The family fulfils a number of functions in Islam and its establishment is also considered a form of worship.

In 1979 a secular theory of income distribution was proposed in which the family was considered key, as both the social unit within which individual incomes are wholly or partially pooled and the means through which abilities, attitudes and property rights are inherited, for it was noted that a function of the large traditional family was the provision of welfare services for its weaker members.[112]

In the Islamic context, the family is defined as a group of people related by blood or marriage, with marriage its central institution. While it is of course fair to acknowledge that there exists a 'gross abuse of Islamic family laws among some uninformed Muslim groups,'[113] it remains the case that all responsibilities regarding the welfare of the family lie with the husband or father. Consequently a man is forbidden from contracting in marriage if he is unable to maintain a family, although there is nothing to prevent a wife who is willing to work from contributing if her husband's income is insufficient to sustain a decent standard of living. Maintenance in the form of the provision of food, clothing, a place of residence, medicine and other essential services is the right of every wife and her children. The Prophet ﷺ said, 'Among the believers who show most perfect faith are those who have the best disposition, and are kindest to their families.'[114]

In theory, resources are not pooled within the Islamic family structure, but are dispersed from a single source. Even if a woman earns her own income or owns property, the responsibility of welfare provision lies with her husband, while she may choose to invest her wealth or use it for personal consumption. It may be suggested that this places a high burden of responsibility on just one family member, particularly in the case of very poor communities, but it is balanced to some degree by the rules of inheritance which take the gender-based contribution into consideration. This is extended further with the recognition that welfare cannot be considered only in financial terms and that welfare provision must be translated into actual family well-being.

When individuals are unable to meet the maintenance targets prescribed by Islamic Law other frameworks come into play. The concept of *zakat* enjoys great prominence within the literature on Islamic economics as it is considered a pillar of Islam along with prayer, fasting and pilgrimage. Normally referred to as obligatory charity, it is the means through which an Islamic government provides for the needs of the desperately poor.

Every Muslim who possesses more than a specified minimum is required to give two and a half per cent of their net wealth as *zakat* to the government. In Pakistan it is discharged by local *zakat* committees which function at the grassroots level.[115] In other areas, particularly where Muslims are in a minority, it is collected from voluntary contributions and distributed by charitable organisations such as *Islamic Relief.*

A number of writers have identified issues with the contemporary implementation of *zakat*, such as its interpretation by modern literalists.[116] It has been noted that some have restricted the commodities covered by *zakat* to those that were identified during the time of the Prophet ﷺ alone despite the fact that in the period that followed, further elements were considered: during the Prophet's ﷺ lifetime, for example, horses were exempt from *zakat*, but by the time of the early Muslim ruler Umar I, it was extended to include them due to the rise of a horse trade. The form of *zakat* proposed by some literalists would serve a major redistributive function only in a primitive agricultural economy, for where no attention is paid to the industrial and service sectors of contemporary economies the burden is met primarily by low-income individuals and not the very wealthy. It has been argued, however, that the sources make the rendering of *zakat* much more inclusive than acknowledged by some contemporary literalists. There is consensus amongst the scholars, for example, that paying *zakat* on stock, merchandise and shares is obligatory.

I firmly believe that religion has an important role to play in modern society. The acquaintance that approached me early one morning with his appeal for all religions to be banned later went on to discuss what he termed the plight of Africa with another colleague, reciting a predictable list of woes: debt, corruption and the spread of Aids. I wondered about the role of religion. The Messenger of God ﷺ warned his community of the deeds that lay the foundation for corruption, injustice and tyranny. Similarly, he told his followers: 'If fornication becomes widespread, then realise that this never happened without new diseases befalling people that their ancestors never suffered from.'[117] We were counselled on the consequences of consuming interest and devouring the rights of others, and have been commanded to give to the poor, to look after widows and orphans, to carry another's burden, to value water and respect the earth. It is, of course, easy to point fingers at the other, but what of our situation?

In 2006, there were 193,700 abortions in England and Wales, a rise of nearly four per cent on the previous year. Across the whole of the United Kingdom approximately 75,000 children are in the care of the state and the responsibility of local authorities—it was estimated that the government would need to spend at least £1.7 billion on foster care in 2006. Domestic violence accounts for 16 per cent of all violent crime in England and Wales and costs in excess of £23 billion per year, not to mention the lives of two women each week. More than two million British children are brought up in families where one or both parents have alcohol problems. Approximately 40 per cent of violent crime, 78 per cent of assaults and 88 of criminal damage cases occur whilst the offender is under the influence of alcohol. There were 139,680 hospital admissions of adults with a diagnosis of mental and behavioural disorders related to alcohol use in the period 2005-6. The total annual healthcare costs related to alcohol misuse is around £1.5 billion. According to figures published by the Bank of England in October 2007, a total of £216 billion was owed in unsecured personal loans and on credit cards in the United Kingdom, a rise of £1.35 billion over the previous month, while the total debt level for consumers had reached £1.38 trillion. The average consumer debt was over £3,000, while the average household debt, excluding mortgages, was almost £9,000.[118] Has man defining who he is and who he wants to be improved the way we live our lives?

Travelling to Turkey over a number of years I found myself largely in the company of loud and often rude secularists who chain-smoked perpetually and frequently declared their dislike for Muslims. Apart from the elderly who still attended the mosque five times a day for prayer, even those Turks who would assign the label 'Muslim' to themselves freely drank alcohol and mocked their brethren with their atheist friends. One such person who was adamant that I sit next to him in the mosque on *Eid* one year, less than 12 hours after he made fun of me for not drinking alcohol, started to exclaim *Al-Fatiha*—the name of the opening chapter of the Qur'an—as a substitute for a swear word whilst watching football. Sure enough, I had met decent Muslims in Turkey, but not many whose teeth still graced their mouths or whose hair had not yet whitened. Instead, most of the people I met who were of my age, younger or into their middle-age followed the path of Ataturk which had become a new religion in its own right. Saddened, my depression came to a head one day whilst staying in a mountain settlement up above the clouds. Sitting in the white-walled mosque I scribbled my thoughts down in minute characters on a scrap of paper:

> I feel frustrated in this once great Muslim land. It seems like the Turks I come into contact with have lost respect for their heritage, their land and themselves. There is no-one under the age of fifty in the mosque—all the faces are aged and wrinkled, mostly ancient as if soon to pass from this world. Instead the middle-aged men spend their days drinking and gambling, mocking the religion of their forefathers. They do not believe in God or the Prophethood of Muhammad, they say; they believe in Ataturk. In respect for this cult they furiously attack the Muslims, ridiculing them to the best of their abilities. They refuse to say *Salam* because it is *Arabca* and insist instead on *Merhaba*, oblivious to its Arabic origin. They do not respect the culture which brought them beautiful mosques, gardens, homes and art—their culture is concrete apartments, satellite football and Raki.
>
> Like their disrespect for their heritage they show how they do not care for their land. All around, the ground is

littered with cans of Efes Pilsen. The streams sourced by natural springs are filled with detritus, plastic bags and cigarette packets. Beneath a sign which reads, 'Water gives life, do not pollute it,' the earth is hidden beneath more cans of beer. It is true that the earth will cleanse itself—when the snow comes in a month's time the streams and land will be washed clean again by the melt that follows it—the huge boulders strewn across this landscape witness to the power of these waters when they come. But how will the people cleanse themselves when they have lost respect for their heritage and their land?

Later during that same visit, however, I caught a glimpse of another Turkey. A young generation of Muslims existed after all and I detected a whisper that there was a living Islam beyond my own community. The stagnation and opposition I had seen thus far was only one face of this once great Muslim land—a land that was once refuge to religious minorities escaping persecution in Europe. On my return two years later I was to discover that some of those hostile characters now fasted and prayed, quietly withdrawing as their friends reignited old arguments.

Frequently we are witness to great battles concerning mere ideas and look on as debates ensue over the definition of the construct of the moment. When our dignity is at stake, we are easily led. We only seek the pleasure of God, we tell ourselves, only for our inward gaze to observe a recurring pattern of response. There will be occasions when we are bombarded with propaganda set on defining for us the realms of civilisation. The best of us wish that its root referred to courtesy and politeness, but know that it does not. Our dictionaries provide a definition that describes an advanced stage or system of human social development. Politeness is, of course, a characteristic of advanced human social development, as is honesty, sincerity, kindness and generosity, but none of these are meant. The stage is set and we will respond accordingly.

I am troubled—I will say—by the fact that the civilised nations are spending vast sums of money on weapons. The United States of America's Department of Defence alone had a budget of $437,111 billion in 2004. While it is true that this expenditure accounted for only four per cent of gross domestic product, its 2005 military budget was still greater than the combined total of the next 27 countries.

Interestingly, the United Kingdom—tiny beside the United States, China and Russia—spends almost as much as Japan and only slightly less than Russia and China: a figure close to $50 billion. The joint expenditure of these nations is 50 times greater than the combined total of Cuba, Iran, Iraq, Libya, North Korea, Sudan and Syria—those famous members of the 'axis of evil'—and contributes to two-thirds of the total expenditure of the entire planet. In the case of the United States, these figures exclude their actions in Iraq and Afghanistan which are funded outside the Federal Budget.[119]

Why—I will grumble—are the civilised nations spending billions on killing machines and on developing the most hideous weapons ever conceived? Consider the BLU-82B/C-130 weapon system, nicknamed Commando Vault in Vietnam and Daisy Cutter in Afghanistan.[120] This is a 15,000-pound bomb based on explosive sludge that is dropped from high altitude to destroy an area between 300 and 900 feet radius. Or consider Fuel-Air Explosives which disperse an aerosol cloud of fuel which is ignited by an embedded detonator to produce an explosion that causes high overpressure. What kind of mind could conceive of such weapons—I will ask—and what sort of nation would fund them? In response to the latest assault on us, we will rush to our own defence with words like these.

Blessed are the meek, says the Bible, for they shall inherit the earth. A time comes when we realise that the labels assigned by those around us are worthless. Spending $500 billion—even $50 billion—on a war machine is not indicative of advanced human social development. Let the primitive nations rejoice: blessed are the humble, for they shall inherit the earth.

'Don't burden yourself with those prayers,' my relative advised me, 'for it will only count against you.' I acknowledged those words patiently, but I did not take them to heart, for I have no idea when will come the moment my lungs no longer expand and my eyes no longer view the world around me. I have always found a way to fit them in, whether hiding in an empty meeting room or hurrying to a mosque in my lunch hour; for half of the year only the midday prayer falls within working hours. I could not afford a moment longer, I insisted, for my whole future was indeed at stake.

The prayer sums up my relationship with every deed enjoined upon the Muslims. Someone else could say that I should take to drinking alcohol for the sake of my career because it lies at the heart of effective networking between colleagues. Another person could say that my abstention from taking interest will only disadvantage me as I grow older. People could say anything, but my position would remain the same. 'So if your religion asked you to blow yourself up,' challenged another relative of mine one day, 'I suppose you'd do that too.' No, I replied, for the Law is not a collection of hypothetical scenarios: it holds that suicide is *haram*, while its ruling on the use of a bomb as a weapon—the medieval precedents were the use of catapults and Greek fire—is that it is also *haram* if it is used in a place where there are civilians because it kills and maims indiscriminately[121]

To worship God is to obey Him. He knows what is best for us, for He is the Creator of all things. We know that 6,500 light-years from Earth, stars are being forged in a tower of dust and gas—smoke in the words of the Qur'an—57 trillion miles high, but this stellar spire is only one structure amidst millions of other nebulae and galaxies, hanging with such beauty beneath the first heaven. When one truly reflects upon His creation— with today's technology the most distant galaxies visible to us are around 12 billion light-years from Earth—we can only conclude that none is worthy of worship except God. To strive in God's way is the only response that appears worthy, insignificant as it may seem in the grand scheme of life. We strive obediently in God's way because it is the closest we come to worshipping Him in the manner that He deserves.

CHAPTER SEVEN

To Honour God

This short book has been a long time in the making and has passed through numerous iterations, surviving every change of heart and period of stagnation. It began as a work entitled, *My Journey*, which remains apt for this describes the approach of each of us to our Creator. We find the journey in the religious imagery of our two traditions: 'Guide us along the straight path,' recites the Muslim in every prayer, while the Christian reads from the scriptures, 'But small is the gate and narrow the road that leads to life, and only a few find it.'[122] In my own case, I began these notes with the sentiment that when I came to believe in Islam in 1998 it was not the end of the road, but rather its beginning.

Two years ago I renamed this book, *Reconciling the Heart*, for this too described my journey towards God. Yet although I am still fond of that title, I settled in the end for the name at the head of this chapter and on the cover of this book: *To Honour God*. For many years—even as a wavering agnostic—my constant refrain has been the notion that I only want to honour God, and so the imagery of the journey returns for I have made little progress in this regard, taking only a few steps along this path.

It is a journey that begins with us turning to God as we sincerely call ourselves to account: there comes a time when we realise that we want to be close to God and there can be no substitute. Thus, responding to the call of our heart, we bring ourselves before Him, repenting for every wrong action that passed before and dedicating ourselves to this path: to worship

God as if we see Him, knowing that truly He sees us. For me, it means to turn in repentance, to strive to purify my heart from its spiritual diseases, to conquer the calls of my lower self and to adhere to God's commands. I find myself with a great need to accomplish humility in prayer and to enjoy true focus, to ward off pride and arrogance, and to replace self-centredness with a life revolving around God, recognising that good works are a means to an end, but not an end in themselves. All of this—I believe—is encapsulated in those six oft-repeated words of mine: I only want to honour God.

The path of Muhammad ﷺ—the religion of Islam—enjoins upon its followers remembrance of God, which means glorifying, exalting and praising Him. In the Qur'an we read, 'Remember Me and I will remember you.'[123] Elsewhere we read, '...and remember your Lord much and glorify Him in the evening and in the early morning.'[124] Another verse reads, 'Those who believe, and whose hearts find their rest in the remembrance of God—for, verily, in the remembrance of God hearts find rest.'[125]

The Prophet ﷺ said, 'The difference between the one who remembers God and the one who does not remember God is like the difference between the living and the dead.'[126] It is also reported that he taught that God says:

As my servant thinks about Me so will I be for him. I am with him if he will remember Me. If he calls on Me by himself I will call him by Myself, and if he calls on Me in a group of people, I mention him in a better group in My presence. If he approaches Me one hand-span, I will approach him one arm's length; if he approaches Me one arm's length, I will approach him by a cubit; if he comes to Me walking, I will come to him running.[127]

For every tiny action on our part, God promises that He will return it with something better. If we turn to Him walking, He will come to us running, for He is indeed the Most Merciful. Even if our sins were like mountains, reaching the clouds of the sky, He promises us forgiveness if we turn to Him alone with sincere repentance. With gifts like these, what excuse do we have not to honour Him?

The Prophet Muhammad ﷺ said, 'Any activity not begun with the words, "In the Name of God, the Compassionate, the Merciful," is severed from its blessings.'[128] He also taught that the deeds most loved by God are those done regularly, even if they are small.

He used to sleep during the earlier part of the night and stood in prayer during the latter part, for he said that the best prayer after those that are obligatory is the prayer at that time. He once said, 'Getting up at night is enjoined upon you, for it was the practice of the pious before you. It brings you near to your Lord and is atonement for evil deeds and a restraint from sin.'[129]

Concerning the ritual prayers performed five times each day, the Messenger ﷺ said, 'If there was a river at the door of the house of one of you, and he bathed in it five times every day, would you say that any dirt would be left on him?' His companions replied that no dirt would be left at all. 'So that is the example of the five prayers by which God washes away sins,' he said.[130] Once he was asked which deed was most loved by God and he replied, 'Prayer which is performed on time.'[131]

The Prophet ﷺ used to seek God's forgiveness and turn to Him in repentance more than 70 times a day. He told us, 'No trouble befalls a Muslim, and no illness, no sorrow, no grief, no harm, no distress, not even a thorn pricks him, without God expiating by it some of his sins.'[132] A man asked him, 'Which part of Islam is best?' He replied, 'To provide food and to say *salam*—peace—to those you know and to those you do not know.'[133] In another narration he said, 'Indeed the nearest people to God are those who begin by saying *salam*.'[134]

The Messenger of God ﷺ said, 'Charity is due upon every limb of a human being each day that the sun rises. To act justly between two people is charity. To help a man with his ride, or to load his provisions on it or lift them up for him is charity. A good word is charity. Every step going to prayer is charity. Removing from the road that which causes harm is charity.'[135] Once he said, 'While a man was walking along, he came across a thorny branch on the way and he removed it. God praised him for that and forgave him his sins.'[136] He taught us, 'Fear God wherever you are; let an evil deed be followed by a good deed so that you blot it out; and be well-behaved towards people.'[137]

Our Prophet ﷺ said, 'Beware of envy, for envy devours good deeds like fire devours firewood.'[138] He also said, 'The strong man is not the one who is strong in wrestling, but the one who controls himself in anger.'[139] The Messenger of God ﷺ never used obscene talk, nor did he listen to it. He taught us to be humble so that no one boasts over his neighbour nor oppresses him. 'None of my companions should tell me anything about anyone,' he said, 'for I like to meet you with a clean heart.'[140] He told his followers, 'Do not talk for a long time without remembering God, for talking much without remembering God is hardness of the heart. The most distant from God amongst mankind is the one with a hardened heart.'[141]

The Prophet ﷺ said, 'The Merciful One shows mercy to those who are themselves merciful to others. So show mercy to whatever is on earth, then He who is in heaven will show mercy to you.'[142] He taught, 'He who does not thank people does not thank God.'[143] He also said, 'When someone has had good done to him and says to the doer, "May God reward you," he has done the utmost praise.'[144] He said that a man does not truly believe until he likes for his brother what he likes for himself.

The word Islam means submission to the will of God and obedience to His Law. Within the teachings of the religion it is defined as the Middle Way, embracing both the Law and its spirit, denying both the Christian's rejection of the Law in favour of its essence and the Pharisee's dismissal of the spirit in favour of devotion to detailed legislation. The Middle Way provides balance so that we may appreciate the wisdom inherent in this way of life.

I often make fun of the eating habits of the Hemsinli people who reside in Artvin Province, Turkey—the ethnic group to which my wife belongs—but really I am only joking. I make fun of their taste for Black Sea Cabbage, for every meal seems to involve this pale-leafed brassica, and I am often heard running off a list part truthful, part made up: boiled cabbage, cabbage *dolma*, cabbage *kofta*, cabbage soup, cabbage fried with onion, pickled cabbage and so on. It is a variation on the old yarn about the Englishman's love for the potato: baked potato, boiled potato, roast potato, mashed potato, potato chips, potato waffles and potato crisps. Yet in truth I have a lot of respect for those who have managed to maintain their traditional diet, warding off the endless possibilities of consumerism. Cabbage and *Hamsi*—the prince of all fish known to the Turks—is my staple diet whenever I go to stay in our village in that forested valley several miles inland from Hopa. Meat is hardly ever eaten and I have a feeling that this is how it should be.

It is sometimes said that the traditional English dish is 'meat and two veg', but in fact the meat element only has a history spanning a few hundred years. Cabbage was probably a staple of the English diet for epochs as well, a prospect unbearable to us in our modern age given our love of meat and variety. Not only are we used to great choice on the culinary front, but we have also come to expect and demand it. We live in a society which has made food one great plank of consumerism and sadly—it seems—many Muslims have fallen for this modern *sunna*, adopting the norms that surround us without question.

Vegetarian Muslims are sometimes lambasted for their abstention from the consumption of meat—some zealous individuals even go as far as to say that not eating meat is *haram*. Yet it seems to me that vegetarians are much closer to the *sunna* of our religion than most of us. In the olden days, wealthy Muslims used to eat meat once a week, while poor Muslims would consume it on the *Eids*. Most of the meals that the Prophet ﷺ ate did not contain meat, and so my friend who eats meat very rarely is simply following the model of the best of us.

I suspect the reason why some Muslims react so strongly to people who eat little meat has less to do with a concern for the prohibitions of our religion and more to do with the desires of our tongues and stomachs. A count of the mostly Muslim-run fried chicken shops along the length of the Uxbridge Road from Shepherd's Bush in London to Uxbridge out west tell us of an insatiable demand. The delightful spread of the generous host for his guests is almost always a lavish stream of *birianis* and curries, chicken, lamb and mountains of meat-laced rice. The daily filling and emptying of the counters in the *halal* butchers tells us that we are a people who really do 'do meat'.

Perhaps, though, we should control ourselves and 'do meat' a little less, in light of this *hadith* recorded in the *Muwatta* of Imam Malik: 'Beware of meat, because it has an addiction like the addiction of wine.' In today's era, however, our problem does not only lie with addiction: what will we say about the way our food was farmed, the way the animal was slaughtered, the way it was cleaned and the way it was sold? When I consider the vast acreage of refrigerated units in our supermarkets always fully stocked with plump chickens, I cannot help but find it quite abhorrent. I am not a vegetarian, but this insatiable demand of ours still worries me. One *Eid* I visited a commercial slaughterhouse and was horrified by the production line they operated, but that is how it has to be in a culture that demands meat as much as ours. When I was studying Development, one of our lecturers—an expert in water politics—predicted that the next war in the Middle East would be over water. He may not have predicted the intervention of a non-regional army seeking out *Weapons of Mass Distraction*, but he made a strong case nevertheless. The production of the tons of grain required to rear animals is dependent on the availability of adequate supplies of water.

In our household, our consumption of meat has lessened somewhat. Some days we eat wholly vegetarian dishes, some days an egg quiche, some days some trout or sea fish and, yes, sometimes some lamb, goat or chicken. Though eating meat is permitted, Muslims are commanded to treat animals kindly, not to slaughter them within sight of other animals—not even to speak of it in their presence—and to use the technique that causes them to quickly slip into a state of deep-sleep unconsciousness. Nowadays we buy our meat once a month from a smallholder that takes the welfare of animals seriously and slaughters on the small scale, taking the kind of care that is impossible on a production line.

There has always been wisdom in the saying that we are what we eat, whether we like it or not. If we care about our spiritual well-being, we must realise that religion has much to say about the food we eat. There is great wisdom in every one of the teachings of Islam and in the words of our Prophet ﷺ. For every piece of advice it is easy to find a reason just by reflecting on our own experiences in our day to day lives.

'O Tongue,' I lamented one summer upon returning from a friend's wedding, 'what on earth is wrong with you?' I was reflecting on a disastrous attempt to socialise with old friends and new. 'Why do you not have the fluency of these typing fingers?' I asked, 'Why do you stutter and break, and disconnect with freely flowing thoughts? What have I done that makes you whisper in good company, what have I done to make you falter?' I wondered if I had neglected my tongue, noting that for months my speech had been stuttering and breaking, leaving my thoughts locked within. 'In every gathering you lock and harden,' I told this piece of flesh, 'and all you say with fluency is *Alhamdulillah.*'

Mankind is never satisfied of course. In different circumstances I would blame my tongue for being too loose. Such is the story of my life throughout these years within the Muslim faith. I have always been conscious of words. Even in the earliest years, I noted the discomfort in my soul which came with misplaced utterances. At work for a moment—seeking some common ground with my peers—I complained aloud about a project manager, feeding upon my own manager's cynicism about her abilities. Ten seconds later, having said it, regret filled my mind.

A week earlier my words had been about my manager. It was not a complaint, but a description of an almost accusing question he had asked me which had caused me some offence. Returning from the production room that morning, I engaged in pointless chatter with the office manager until, as if it were a release, the unnecessary repetition slipped off my tongue. There was no need to pass on what he had said to me at all, and so regret struck me again just as I said it. 'What am I doing,' I asked myself?

In days gone by there were words in the *Letter of James* that I appreciated well. I had seen their example in action and felt the pain and the misery that grew from the tiniest spark. 'Think of a ship,' wrote James, 'large though it may be and driven by gales, it can be steered by a very small rudder on whatever course the helmsman chooses. So with the tongue; it is small, but its pretensions are great. What a vast amount of timber can be set ablaze by the tiniest spark!'[145]

It was something that I have always believed in with passion, for I have been cast aside because of rumours and dismissed because of words. Yet repeatedly I have found myself sitting on my own, examining my own soul and recognising that, I too, will occasionally drop a spark when it suits me. We fear alienation from our colleagues, so we join in with their games. We have been done down and we want to get back up. We have been slandered, so we want to get revenge. Or maybe, it is more subtle than that, down in the roots of our intentions: perhaps we want respect and we believe that words will win that prize.

Many of us fall into this trap. I used to read the feedback columns that followed articles on the internet and would often come across the thoughtless ranting of individuals responding to words which did not need to be said with more words which did not need to be said. I would sometimes listen to friends telling me about such and such a person, speaking words which need not have been uttered. Sitting with our friends we tend to take in everything they say to us, because they are our friends. We accept slander of our enemy, because he is our enemy.

'These women, they're no good, because they did this and this…'
'Don't trust that man. He did such and such!' 'Don't talk to him, he's no good.'

Do we ever stop and ask, 'How do you know?' or do we just accept it because our companion told us so? Do we stop and say, 'I don't want to hear this. I'm abandoning your company until you desist'? Do we ever enquire? Do we verify our facts? Will we find out one day that our witness actually only heard it from his friend, who heard it from his friend, who overheard it from some people talking one day, who heard it from a journalist, from a friend who was not even sure and was not even there? Will we find out that our confidante has never even spoken to the woman she deconstructs and scrutinises for our benefit? Will we discover in the end that the man who was convicted a sinner, was in fact more sincere and pious than the best of us? Will we one day find out that we have learned nothing, except that we learned nothing about our companion?

Our blessed Prophet ﷺ said, 'He who truly believes in God and the Last Day should speak good or keep silent.'[146] For those of us who love to write, as well as those who have been granted great speech, the implications of this are clear. To write brings with it responsibilities, generating questions which exercise me constantly. The command to 'speak good' must equally apply to all forms of communication. In the Islamic worldview a word is an act, just as to walk, run or eat is an act, as Gai Eaton made clear:

> In whatever society we may live, our actions are constrained in the public interest and, in Europe and America during the present century, these constraints have multiplied so rapidly that our ancestors, even a hundred years ago, might have found life almost intolerable. The Muslim may reasonably ask how it is that we accept this vast and oppressive network of laws and regulations while, at the same time, removing all constraints from one of the most potent forms of action; the spoken or written word.'[147]

A book, he pointed out, can easily become the indirect cause of genocide, to take an extreme but not unreasonable example. Yet this viewpoint is not even exclusively Islamic—freedom was understood by Kant as the freedom to do good, for example, rather than the freedom to do anything as it is often presented nowadays. To go further, a distinction can be drawn between freedom and rights. Although Islam grants the individual the freedom to say anything, it does not grant him or her the right to slander, backbite or lie—these are considered reprehensible sins.

In English law, limits are placed on the freedom of expression in certain circumstances, such as the need to protect the rights of others, as in defamation, protection of reputation and privacy. National security also constitutes a justification for censorship, along with sedition, public interest, public health, public morals, obscenity, public order, prevention of violence, terrorism, racism, sexism and religious intolerance.

Muslims are a people commanded to speak good or stay silent, and so I wrestle with myself regarding my love of writing, which brings me joy and relief. Whenever I reconcile myself to this passion, I consider it a gift from God. Some are given the eloquence of the tongue, others the hand of the calligrapher. Some are given great strength and energy, others compassionate gentleness. Everyone is given their gift, to be used to the glory of their Creator and His way. Still, that question recurs: is it a gift or is it a test? Is it a tool to be used for good or is it a distraction that replaces God-centredness with the ego? I regularly ponder this question, for I have an ambiguous relationship with the arts, with those nuances of the human condition. On the one hand, my faith inspires me with beauty, while on the other, some Muslims state that true knowledge is our only armoury. Thus I often find myself caught between the desire to put my talents to the service of good and the fear that they may rather lead me astray.

The power of words is astonishing. Some have the power to stir the emotions, to lighten one's load. Others strike like a knitting needle pushed through the heart; that piercing pain that arises on receipt of harsh sentiments. Others still just perturb.

Invite to the way of your Lord with wisdom and beautiful preaching says the Qur'an.[148] I wish we did. Sometimes in our zealous desire to convey a message of beauty, we abandon good manners and common etiquette. I have a friend who spent his early days as a Muslim amongst a particular group of believers until he could take their harsh words no more. Ripping into him with their tongues, they left him in tears in a public gathering more than once. Traumatised by those years, he has left them far behind, but now he has harsh words for them. It is not true that the people of that group are alone in suffering from this disease. I have seen and heard the harsh words of both the *Salafi* and the *Sufi*, the traditionalist and the modernist, the *Sunni* and the *Shia*; indeed I have encountered the callous words of the evangelical Baptist for the Roman Catholic, even of the parochial church council for the priest.

If some of us are remiss, then advise us in the best of ways. If some of us have made mistakes, remind us in a way that is kind. If I do not have knowledge the like of yours, invite me to the way of our Lord with wisdom and beautiful speech. The power of words is indeed astonishing. No wonder we are warned to maintain control of our tongues at all times and of our typing finger by extension. What a vast amount of timber can be set ablaze by the tiniest spark. This does not only refer to the destruction caused by a rumour, for even isolated words can crush the soul. Words can be uplifting, words can be light, words can be a comfort and words can be a guide, but we must evaluate all that falls without. An old Muslim tradition asks us to keep four questions in mind at all times:

'Are these words true?'
'Are these words necessary?'
'Are these words beneficial?'
'Are these words kind?'

Though difficult to achieve to be sure, the advice that follows is that if the answer to any of the questions is no, those words would be best left unspoken and unwritten. No doubt we all make mistakes, but we would be wise to keep those four questions in mind, to take them to heart and live by them.

One Friday evening, taking the time to listen to some worries I had, a teacher of mine told me about a tree in paradise reserved for those who retained criticism only for themselves in life, sparing their neighbours from assault and leaving alone that which did not concern them—a tree providing shade over a distance that would take 80 years to travel. It need not take us long to realise that certain principles are of importance, permeating the teachings of our Prophet ﷺ: our neighbours have rights that include being safe from our tongues; when we give advice, we are commanded to do so with the best of speech; we are told to think before we speak; before taking any action, we are ordered to remove anger, rancour and envy from our hearts.

Contemplation of the food that passes our lips and meditation on the speech of our tongues are merely two aspects related to the way we live our lives. Much could be written about the gaze of our eyes and modesty, or about shunning arrogance and envy. In the Qur'an we read:

> Serve God, and do not join any partners with Him; and do good to parents, kinsfolk, orphans, those in need, neighbours who are near, neighbours who are strangers, the companion by your side, the wayfarer and what your right hands possess: for God does not love the arrogant, the boastful.[149]

Of his mission, the Prophet ﷺ said, 'I was only sent to perfect noble character.'[150] Yet is all this emphasis on perfecting our character and adopting the simple characteristics of religion not futile in this age of extreme conflict? I do not believe it is, for in the Qur'an we read, 'The servants of the Merciful are those who tread lightly on the earth, and when ignorant people deride them, they reply "peace".[151] Here too we find wisdom in our teachings: violent protests and the burning of flags never achieved anything except increasing hatred. Our Prophet ﷺ told us:

> Towards the latter days of indiscriminate violence, be like the first and better of the two sons of Adam who said, 'If you raise your hand to kill me, I will not raise mine to kill you; surely I fear God, the Lord of the worlds.'[152]

It is true that sometimes it can be daunting to define a role for ourselves: we wonder what impact we can make on the world around us as individuals. In an age that demands immediate answers to every problem, the traditional approach of religion can seem tiresome. In Muslim tradition, the internal struggles against the lowest calls of the self were seen as the gateway to prosperity, not protest and sloganeering. For me, confirmation of this truth was found in Scotland's immense beauty.

Whilst staying in Broomhall Castle on the side of the Ochil Hills in Menstrie during my postgraduate studies I used to climb over the fence behind that sandstone building at weekends and ascend vast hills on foot. High up, there were great views of Stirling and the Firth of Forth. Once over the hill I would trample down into the valley and follow the rivers and streams as far as I could.

I learnt a lot from those waters. Sometimes I would encounter a stream that was nothing but a dribble through the grass, sometimes a bubbling brook. Every beck was fed by scores of tiny tributaries and every small river by dozens of streams. In one afternoon I would pass hundreds of watery veins across the fields and rocks, feeding one new watercourse after another. I would ponder on those waterways dribbling down the higher ground at their source, for on my way I had passed the rushing torrent heading out of the valley, carving its way between huge boulders. Across the lowland, through the village, this wide river joined another, that one joining another and on and on, until it joined the glorious shining Firth of Forth far in the distance.

One particular afternoon, while heading onwards further than before, I understood the parable in that magnificent landscape. We are not required to be mighty rivers to get our life's work done. Each of us can contribute to a wider goal by performing even the smallest deed. Some of us are the tiny tributaries feeding the larger streams. Some are energetic brooks feeding the rivers. Some are cascading rivers swelling the wide, deep estuaries. All of us have a role and however insignificant it may seem at the time, it will always make a huge difference in the end.

Emphasis on perfecting our character and adopting the simple characteristics of religion must continue precisely because we live in an age of extreme conflict. We may be derided and mocked by those around us—by fellow believers as much as those without faith—but we recall that our return is to God. One day, we will face the Hour and stand before our Lord, shoulder to shoulder, as in that grand dress-rehearsal on the Plain of Arafat during the annual *hajj*—but on a day the like of which is 50,000 years. It will not matter that day what our fellow travellers thought of us.

There used to be a trend in which converts to Islam would be encouraged to change their name, swapping the moniker given to them by their parents for a Muslim variation. Thus Richard might become Abdullah, meaning Servant of God, and Matthew might become Abdur-Rahman, meaning Servant of the Most Merciful, while Ian might choose Ibrahim, taking on the name of a grand prophet that preceded us. My friends, however, have always insisted on Tim—the name chosen for me by my loving parents. I am glad about that, for looking into the origin of my name one day, tired of a stranger demanding to know why I still called myself this, I learnt that it derives from the Greek *Timotheos* which means, 'To honour God'.

There could be no nobler end for any of us than to be of those that have lived a life that honoured God. I pray that one day I might begin to realise this fine ambition. Between our souls and God lie our hearts and our deeds, and nothing else lies between us.

END NOTES

1   *Hadith* reported in the *sahih* collection of Muslim.

2   Adapted from J Maw, *Twende! A Practical Swahili Course* (Oxford University Press, 1985), p.7.

3   Qur'an 2:255. This verse, known as Ayat al-Kursi, was described by the Prophet Muhammad ﷺ as the greatest in the Qur'an.

4   AJ Arberry, *The Koran Interpreted* (Oxford University Press, 1964), p.491, with reference to Qur'an 41:11.

5   *Ibid*, p.325, with reference to Qur'an 21:30.

6   The 12 types of left-handed amino acids that occur 288 times in a particular protein molecule can be arranged in 10^{300} ways, but only one arrangement linked by peptide bonds is viable—some proteins contain chains of thousands of amino acids. A single human cell is made up of 200,000 types of protein, as well as nucleic acids, carbohydrates, lipids and vitamins. The DNA gene responsible for controlling a single protein made up of 288 amino acids would have around 1,000 nucleotides in its chain, which could occur in 41,000 forms— the probable random formation of such a nucleotide in the correct sequence is one in 10^{600}.

7   Qur'an 52:35.

8   The Letter of James 4:13-17.

9   Deuteronomy 5:7.

10 N Gumbel, *Searching Issues* (Kingsway Publications, 1994), p.30-1.

11 *Hadith* reported in the collections of Tirmidhi and Ahmad.

12 Qur'an 7:37. See also 7:20-23.

13 Qur'an 6:164.

14 *Hadith* reported in the *sahih* collection of Bukhari.

15 H Küng, *Christianity and the World Religions—Paths of Dialogue with Islam, Hinduism and Buddhism* (Doubleday Publishing, 1986), p.24.

16 H J Schoeps, *Theologie und Geschichte des Judenchristentums* (1949, reprinted by Hildesheim 1988), p.342.

17 Vatican scholars, for example, have undertaken some work to incorporate information contained in the *Dead Sea Scrolls* into the biblical text.

18 FJ Badcock, *The History of the Creeds* (SPCK, 1938), p.24.

19 MM Al-Azami, *The History of the Qur'anic Text from Revelation to Compilation* (UKIA, 2003), p.167.

20 Islam is marked out amongst the world religions by the fact that huge numbers of its teachings were related through women. The Prophet's wife Aisha was an outstanding scholar and doctor, famed for her extensive knowledge of the Arabic language and the division of inheritance, who narrated thousands of his sayings and deeds. Other women such as Hafsa, Maymuna, Umm Habiba and Umm Salama are also well known as transmitters of *hadith*. Biographical dictionaries provide a rich source of information about the great number of women involved in transmitting *hadith* over several hundred years.

21 MM Al-Azami, *The History of the Qur'anic Text from Revelation to Compilation* (UKIA, 2003), p.185.

22 MA Anees and AN Athar, *Guide to Sira and Hadith Literature in Western Languages* (Mansell Publishing, 1986), p.xiii.

23 DF Eickelman and JW Anderson, 'Publishing in Muslim countries: less censorship, new audiences and rise of the 'Islamic' book' in *LOGOS* (Whurr Publishers, 1997), 8/4.

24 F Rosenthal, *Knowledge Triumphant: The Concept of Knowledge in Medieval Islam* (EJ Brill, 1970), p.19.

25 M Watt, *What is Islam?* (Longman, Green and Company, 1968), pp.124-125.

26 B Lewis, *Islam in History* (Open Court Publishing, 1993), pp.104-105.

27 W Moberly, *Can Balaam's Ass Speak Today? A Case Study in Reading the Old Testament as Scripture* (Grove Books, 1998), p.3.

28 B Metzger, *The Canon Of The New Testament: Its Origin, Significance & Development* (Clarendon Press, 1997), pp.305-315.

29 *ibid.* pp.187-188.

30 *ibid.* pp.241-245.

31 From Qur'an 16:36.

32 The opening chapter of the Qur'an, 1:1-7.

33 *Hadith* recorded in *Al-Adab al-Mufrad* of Bukhari.

34 Qur'an 13:11.

35 Qur'an 91:1-10.

36 *Hadith* reported in the *sahih* collections of Bukhari and Muslim.

37 Qur'an 25:70.

38 *Hadith* recorded in the *sahih* collection of Bukhari.

39 *Hadith* recorded in the *sahih* collection of Muslim and explained in an-Nawawi's *Forty Hadith*: '…The Messenger of God said, "Islam is that you witness that there is no god but God and that Muhammad is the Messenger of God, and you establish the prayer, and you give the *zakat* and you fast Ramadan, and you perform the *hajj* of the House if you are able to take a way to it…'

40 Some observers suspected that such unsavoury political machinations continue to occur in our own times after two SAS servicemen in civilian dress—charged with killing five or nine inhabitants—were arrested in Basra, Iraq in September 2005. It was alleged that their Toyota Cressida was found to contain weapons, explosives and a remote-control detonator, while initial reports claimed they were dressed as Arabs. It has since been reported, however, that the men were engaged in undercover surveillance of senior Iraqi police officers suspected of being behind a series of attacks on British troops. God knows best.

41 *Hadith* recorded in the collections of Ahmad and Tirmidhi.

42 *Hadith* recorded in the *sahih* collection of Muslim.

43 As in a *hadith* recorded in the collection of Ahmed, '…the strong will devour the weak, until the Hour comes' and of Abu Dawud, 'The nations will summon each other upon you as you call guests to eat from a plate of food…'

44 In Islamic Law, various dispensations exist to cover unusual circumstances, such as the permission to consume foods that are ordinarily considered *haram* when one is faced with starvation.

45 It is estimated that close to 50 million people died during the course of *World War Two* alone.

46 J Muldoon, *Popes, Lawyers and Infidels: The Church and the Non-Christian World 1250-1550* (Liverpool University Press, 1979), p.134.

47 M Sells, *The Bridge Betrayed: Religion and genocide in Bosnia* (University of California Press, 1996), p.144.

48 *Ibid.* p.85.

49 A Hastings, *The Shaping of Prophecy: Passion, Perception and Practicality* (Geoffrey Chapman, 1995), p.151.

50 M Ipgrave, *The Road Ahead: A Christian-Muslim Dialogue* (Church House Publishing, 2002), p.ix.

51 Qur'an 2:190.

52 Qur'an 8:61.

53 Qur'an 9:5. Classical exegeses of the verse by Muslim Scholars include qualifiers such as 'specifically, those who have breached the Treaty', 'those who have declared war against you' and 'specifically, the *Jahili* Arabs and not anyone else'. Quoted in MA Al-Akiti, *Defending the Transgressed by Censuring the Reckless Against the Killing of Civilians—Fatwa Against the Targeting of Civilians* (2005), p.31.

54 From a *hadith* recorded in the collections of Ahmad, Ibn Majah, Abu Dawud, Tirmidhi and others.

55 MA Al-Akiti, *Defending the Transgressed by Censuring the Reckless Against the Killing of Civilians—Fatwa Against the Targeting of Civilians* (2005), pp.30-44.

56 *Ibid.* p.45.

57 Gospel of Luke 6:42.

58 Gospel of Matthew 7:18 and Gospel of Luke 6:43.

59 H Yusuf, *Islam has a progressive tradition too* (The Guardian, 19 June 2002).

60 M Percy and I Jones (eds.), *Fundamentalism, Church and Society* (SPCK, 2002), p.148.

61 In fact I know Muslims of Sikh and Hindu descent as well, but that is another story.

62 It is nevertheless right that we acknowledge our indebtedness to the immigrant Muslim communities that went to the trouble of establishing mosques at their own expense, despite the economic deprivation that many of them faced. It is also true that our failure to attend the mosque regularly for the other prayers throughout the week is an impediment to inclusiveness; we have a role to play too.

63 *Hadith* recorded in the collection of Ahmad.

64 M Duggan, *When the chips are down* (Church Times, 31 July 1998), p.4.

65 From a *hadith* reported in the collection of Ahmad: 'Forgive him who wrongs you; join him who cuts you off; do good to him who does bad to you; and speak the truth even if it be against yourself.'

66 *Hadith* reported in the collection of Abu Dawud.

67 It is prohibited for enemy soldiers to be killed cruelly or by burning, to be subjected to torture or to be put to death after being bound. Muslim soldiers are forbidden to loot or touch any civilian or non-combatant property, to slaughter their livestock for food or take the milk from their cattle, to fell fruit bearing trees or to burn or destroy the enemy's crops. It is also prohibited for Muslims to fight without warning or ultimatum, or to launch a nightly attack when people may be asleep.

68 Quoted from 1 Corinthians 11:5. See also 1 Corinthians 11:3-16 and 14:34-35 for example.

69 Qur'an 91:1-10.

70 *Sharia*—meaning 'way'—is a comprehensive body of law which is divided into two sections: acts of worship and human interactions. The former includes ritual purification, prayers, fasting, charity and pilgrimage, while the latter covers financial transactions, laws of inheritance, endowments, marriage, child care, food and judicial matters. When asked if they believe in *sharia*, most Muslims will have in mind this broad corpus of guidance.

71 While chastising the behaviour of flag-made-of-tissue-burning, sanction-wielding Muslims overseas, we appeared to have forgotten the 500,000 Iraqi children that the *United Nations Children's Fund* estimated died as a result of the sanctions imposed on the country after the Gulf War of 1990.

72 According to the US Department of State's *Country Reports on Human Rights Practices–2007* released by the *Bureau of Democracy, Human Rights, and Labor* on 11 March 2008, almost 100 Muslim graves in Venstre Kirkegaard cemetery in Copenhagen were desecrated in 2005, while more than 20 Muslim graves were desecrated in a cemetery in Esbjerg in February 2006. In November that year markers indicating where Muslim graves were to be situated were removed and replaced with pig heads on poles. In 2005 *Radio Holger* was closed by authorities for three months, but continued broadcasting via the internet.

73 *Hadith* reported in the *sahih* collection of Bukhari. Commenting on this *hadith* the famous scholar, Suyuti, wrote that it means, 'do not act in accordance with what your anger makes you incline towards, and restrain yourself. As for anger itself, a human cannot prevent it; rather, what they can prevent is acting in according to what anger calls one to do.'

74 Qur'an 33:35.

75 Dr Wafa Sultan quoted by M Charen, *Stand up: Wafa Sultan* (townhall.com, 17 March 2006).

76 N Matar, *Islam in Britain: 1558-1685* (Cambridge University Press, 1998).

77   From *Seeking asylum from the past* (The
      Neurocentric, 30 December 1997).

78   Qur'an 49:13.

79   Qur'an 3:103.

80   Qur'an 2:152.

81   *Hadith* recorded in the *sahih* collection
      of Muslim.

82   Qur'an 15:56.

83   Qur'an 39:53.

84   *Hadith* recorded in the collection of
      Ibn Majah.

85   Qur'an 29:2.

86   Paul's Letter to the Galatians 3:11.

87   Gospel of Matthew 5:18.

88   A Ghazali and S Omar (eds.), *Readings
      in the Concept and Methodology of Islamic
      Economics* (Pelanduk Publications,
      1989), p.10.

89   AM Sadeq, *Economic Development in
      Islam* (Pelanduk Publications, 1990), p.1.

90   K Marx, *Contributions to the Critique of
      Hegel's Philosophy of Law*, quoted in J
      Elster (ed.), *Karl Marx: a Reader*
      (Cambridge University Press, 1986),
      p.301.

91   *Ibid.*

92   V Lenin, *On Religion* (Moscow:
      Progress Publishers, 1978), p.8.

93   E Wax, *Islam Attracting Many Survivors of
      Rwanda Genocide—Jihad Is Taught as
      'Struggle to Heal'* (Washington Foreign
      Post Service, 23 September 2002),
      p.A10.

94   PQ Ufford and M Schoffeleers (eds.),
      *Religion and Development: Towards an
      Integrated Approach* (Free University
      Press, 1988), p.167.

95   P Gifford, *Christian Fundamentalism and
      Development* (Review of African
      Political Economy 52, 1991), p.11.

96   P Hall, *Growth and Development: An
      Economic Analysis* (Oxford: Martin
      Robertson, 1983), p.4.

97   MP Todaro, *Economic Development*
      (Longman, 1997), p.609.

98   AM Sadeq, *Economic Development in
      Islam* (Pelanduk Publications, 1990), p.5.

99   S George, *A Fate Worse than Debt*
      (Penguin Books, 1994), p.27.

100   B Hume, *Forgive the poorest their debts—
      now* (The Times, 14 May 1998).

101   See Exodus 22:25; Leviticus 25:36;
      Psalms 15:5; Ezekiel 18:8 and 18:13.
      Also JDM Derrett, *Loans and Interest* in
      DM Metzger and MD Coogan (eds.),
      The Oxford Companion to the Bible
      (Oxford University Press, 1993), p.463.

102   Luke 6:35. Also *Encyclical of Pope
      Benedict XIV* promulgated on 1
      November 1745 at St. Mary Major,
      Rome (www.ewtn.com/library).

103   Qur'an 2:275.

104   *Hadith* recorded in the collection of
      Tirmidhi.

105   M Rodinson, *Islam and Capitalism*
      (Penguin Books, 1974), p.14 and T
      Kuran in KS Jomo (ed.), *Islamic Economic
      Alternatives. Critical Perspectives and New
      Directions* (Macmillan, 1992), p.27.

106   *Hadith* recorded in the collection of
      Abu Dawud.

107   L Boxberger, *Avoiding Riba: Credit and
      Custodianship in Nineteenth- and Early-
      Twentieth Century Hadramawt* (Islamic
      Law and Society 5/2, 1998), p.196.

108   Kuran in KS Jomo (ed.), *Islamic Economic
      Alternatives. Critical Perspectives and New
      Directions* (Macmillan, 1992), p.31.

109   R Charles and D Maclaren, *The Social
      Teachings of Vatican II: Its Origin and
      Development—Catholic Social Ethics: an
      historical and comparative study* (Plater
      Publications, 1982), p.334 detailing
      Populorum Progressio, the Encyclical Of
      Pope Paul VI, *On The Development Of
      Peoples*, 26 March 1967.

110   F Stewart, *Basic Needs Strategies, Human
      Rights, and the Right to Development*
      (Human Rights Quarterly 11, 1989),
      p.347.

111   *Waqf* trust institutions, for example,
      funded the establishment and
      administration of hospitals and schools
      from the seventh century onwards.
      Some commentators have noted its
      similarities to English trust law, which
      may have been influenced by the *waqf*
      institutions encountered during the
      Crusades of the twelfth and thirteenth
      centuries.

112 H Lydall, *A Theory of Income Distribution* (Clarendon Press, 1979), p.265.

113 AR Omran, *Family Planning in the Legacy of Islam* (Routledge, 1992), p.40.

114 *Hadith* reported in the collection of Tirmidhi.

115 SA Peerzade, *The Definition and Measurement of Poverty: An Integrated Islamic Approach* (The Pakistan Development Review 36/1, 1997), p.93.

116 Y Qaradawi, *Islamic Awakening between Rejection and Extremism* (The International Institute of Islamic Thought, 1993), pp.53-54 and T Kuran in KS Jomo (ed.), *Islamic Economic Alternatives. Critical Perspectives and New Directions* (Macmillan, 1992), pp.22-23.

117 From a longer *hadith* in the collection of Ibn Majah.

118 All of these figures are taken from published *Home Office, National Health Service*, Local Government and *Bank of England* reports.

119 See for example the *SIPRI Year Book 2007*, the *CIA World Factbook 2008* and the *World Military Expenditures and Arms Transfers* report.

120 *The Federation of American Scientists, Military Analysis Network* (www.fas.org/man/dod-101)

121 MA Al-Akiti, *Defending the Transgressed by Censuring the Reckless Against the Killing of Civilians—Fatwa Against the Targeting of Civilians* (2005), p.28.

122 Qur'an 1:6 and Gospel of Matthew 7:14.

123 Qur'an 2:152.

124 From Qur'an 3:41.

125 Qur'an 13:28.

126 *Hadith* reported in the *sahih* collection of Bukhari.

127 *Hadith* reported in the *sahih* collections of Bukhari and Muslim.

128 *Hadith* reported in the collection of Abu Dawud.

129 *Hadith* reported in the collection of Tirmidhi.

130 *Hadith* reported in the *sahih* collection of Bukhari.

131 *Hadith* reported in the *sahih* collection of Bukhari.

132 *Hadith* reported in the *sahih* collections of Bukhari and Muslim.

133 *Hadith* reported in the *sahih* collection of Bukhari.

134 *Hadith* reported in the collections of Tirmidhi, Abu Dawud and Ahmad.

135 *Hadith* reported in the *sahih* collections of Bukhari and Muslim.

136 *Hadith* reported in the *sahih* collection of Bukhari.

137 *Hadith* reported in the collections of Tirmidhi and Ahmad.

138 *Hadith* reported in the collection of Abu Dawud.

139 *Hadith* reported in the *sahih* collections of Bukhari and Muslim.

140 *Hadith* reported in the collection of Abu Dawud.

141 *Hadith* reported in the collection of Tirmidhi.

142 *Hadith* reported in the collections of Tirmidhi and Abu Dawud.

143 *Hadith* reported in the collections of Tirmidhi and Ahmad.

144 *Hadith* reported in the collection of Tirmidhi.

145 The Letter of James 3:6.

146 *Hadith* recorded in the *sahih* collections of Bukhari and Muslim.

147 G Eaton, *Islam and the Destiny of Man* (The Islamic Texts Society, 1998), pp.40-41.

148 Qur'an 16:125.

149 Qur'an 4:36.

150 *Hadith* recorded in the collection of Ahmad and the *Muwatta*.

151 Qur'an 25:63.

152 From a *Hadith* recorded in the collection of Tirmidhi.

GLOSSARY

ﷺ: A salutation meaning, 'Peace and blessings of God be upon him' used after the Prophet Muhammad's name.

عليه السلام: A salutation meaning, 'Peace be upon him' used after the names of other prophets and messengers.

Adhan: The call made by a Muslim man for prayer.

Alhamdulilah: All praise be to God.

Allah: Name of the Creator of all the worlds and whatever is contained in them.

Dawa: Medicine in Swahili.

Dhikr: Remembering God, either with the words of the tongue or within one's heart.

Eid: A festival, marking either the end of Ramadan or the pilgrimage.

Hadith: A saying of or about the Prophet Muhammad ﷺ.

Hadith Qudsi: A saying attributed to God by the Prophet ﷺ which is not part of the Qur'an.

Halal: Whatever is lawful according to Islamic jurisprudence.

Hamd: Praise.

Haram: Whatever is unlawful according to Islamic jurisprudence.

Hijab: A veil or headscarf.

Iftar: The meal that breaks the fast, usually just after sunset.

Ijazah: A written or verbal permission given by a teacher to his or her student to transmit their learning.

Insha'Allah: If God wills.

Isnad: Chain of transmission.

Istikarah: Asking for what is good from God when one is not sure in choosing between things.

Kerygma: The essence of Christian apostolic preaching.

Mujahideen: Those who fight in the way of God according to His laws.

Nikab: A piece of fabric that covers a woman's face.

Rahim: Most merciful, specifically in granting a continuous stream of blessings.

Rahman: Most merciful, specifically by creating.

Ramadan: A lunar calendar month during which Muslims fast from daybreak to sunset.

Riba: Usury.

Sahih: Authentic in the science of *hadith* or correct in jurisprudence.

Salam: Peace.

Salams: Slang used by English-speaking Muslims to describe the greetings of peace exchanged between Muslims.

Salat: Formal prayer during which verses of the Qur'an are recited, that starts with the words, 'God is Great' and includes bowing and prostration.

Sharia: A comprehensive body of religious law defining acts of worship and human interactions.

Shukr: Being grateful in thoughts, words and actions.

Sira: Biography.

Subhanallah: Exalted is God.

Sunna: The words, actions and attributes of the Prophet ﷺ as well as the words, actions and attributes of others commented on by the Prophet ﷺ.

Tahajud: Night prayer other than the obligatory ones.

Tawbah: Repentance.

Tawhid: Attesting to the oneness of God.

Yayla: Turkish highlands.

Zakat: A portion of one's wealth that is given by a Muslim to the needy.

BIBLIOGRAPHY

Abbott, WM (1966) *The Documents of Vatican II* (Association Press)

Al-Afendi, MH and Baloch, NA eds. (1980) *Curriculum and Teacher Education* (Hodder and Stoughton)

Al-Akiti, MA (2005) *Defending the Transgressed by Censuring the Reckless Against the Killing of Civilians—Fatwa Against the Targeting of Civilians*

Al-Attas, SN ed. (1979) *Aims and Objectives of Islamic Education* (Hodder and Stoughton)

Al-Azami, MM (1985) *On Schacht's Origins of Islamic Jurisprudence* (John Wiley and Sons)

Al-Azami, MM (2003) *The History of The Qur'anic Text from Revelation to Compilation* (UKIA)

Al-Faruqi, IR (1988) *Islam and Other Faiths* (The Islamic Foundation)

Al-Faruqi, IR (1992) *Al-Tawhid: Its Implications for Thought and Life* (IIIT)

Al-Khattab, H (1997) *Bent Rib: A Journey Through Women's Issues in Islam* (Ta-Ha)

Allen, T and Thomas, A eds. (1992) *Poverty and Development in the 1990s* (Oxford University Press)

Amirouche, H (1998) Algeria's Islamist Revolution: The People Versus Democracy? *Middle East Policy* 6/1

Anees, MA and Athar, AN (1986) *Guide to Sira and Hadith Literature in Western Languages* (Mansell Publishing Limited)

An-Nawawi (1998) *The Complete Forty Hadith* (Ta-Ha)

Arberry, A J (1964) *The Koran Interpreted* (Oxford University Press)

Arthur, CJ (1970) *Karl Marx and Frederick Engels: The German Ideology* (Lawrence and Wishart)

Article 19 (1991) *Information, Freedom and Censorship World Report* (Library Association Publishing)

Asad, M (1954) *The Road to Mecca* (Simon & Schuster)

Azami, MM (1978) *Studies in Early Hadith Literature: with a Critical Edition of some Early Texts* (American Trust Publications)

Badcock, FJ (1938) *The History of the Creeds* (SPCK)

Banner, JM (1988) 'Preserving the integrity of peer review' in *Journal of Scholarly Publishing* (University of Toronto Press) 19/2

Barr, J (1988) 'Abba, Father', in *Theology*, Vol.91, No.741

Bernstein, H (1992) *Rural Livelihoods: Crises and Responses* (Oxford University Press)

Bible (1978) *Revised Standard Version* (Oxford University Press and Cambridge University Press)

Boxberger, L (1998) Avoiding Riba: Credit and Custodianship in Nineteenth- and Early-Twentieth Century Hadramawt. *Islamic Law and Society* 5/2.

Brown, D (1985) *The Divine Trinity* (Duckworth)

Bukhari (2005) *Al-Adab Al-Mufrad—A Code for Everyday Living: The Example of the Early Muslims* (UKIA)

Chapra, MU (1992) *Islam and the Economic Challenge* (The Islamic Foundation)

Charen, M (17 March 2006) *Stand up: Wafa Sultan* (townhall.com)

Charles, R and Maclaren, D (1982) *The Social Teachings of Vatican II: Its Origin and Development–Catholic Social Ethics: an historical and comparative study* (Plater Publications)

Church of England (1980) *The Alternative Service Book* (SPCK)

Clark, G (1934) *The Later Stuarts 1660-1714* (Oxford University Press)

Comfort, PW (1990) *Early Manuscripts & Modern Translations of the New Testament* (Baker Book House)

Davies, G (1959) *The Early Stuarts 1603-1660* (Oxford University Press)

De George, RT and Woodward, F (1994) 'Ethics and Manuscript Reviewing' in *Journal of Scholarly Publishing* (University of Toronto Press) 25/3

Denffer, AV (1979) *A Day With The Prophet* (The Islamic Foundation)

Derricourt, RM (1996) *An Author's Guide to Scholarly Publishing* (Princeton University Press)

Doi, AR (1984) *Shari'ah: The Islamic Law* (Ta-Ha)

Duggan, M (31 July 1998) *When the chips are down* (Church Times)

Dunn, JDG (1980) *Christiology in the Making* (SCM Press)

Eaton, G (1998) *Islam and the Destiny of Man* (The Islamic Texts Society)

Edens, DG (1979) *Oil and Development in the Middle East* (Praeger Publishers)

Eickelman, DF and Anderson, JW (1997) 'Publishing in Muslim countries: less censorship, new audiences and rise of the "Islamic" book' in *LOGOS* (Whurr Publishers Ltd.) 8/4

Eid, F (1994) Studies of Islam, Economics and Governance: A Survey of Some New Developments. *The American Journal of Islamic Social Sciences* 11/1

Elliot, C (1971) *The Development Debate* (SCM Press)

Elster, J ed. (1986) *Karl Marx: a Reader* (Cambridge University Press)

Findlay, AM (1994) *The Arab World* (Routledge)

Funk, R and Hoover, R (1993) *The Five Gospels: What Did Jesus Really Say?* (Macmillan)

George, S (1994) *A Fate Worse than Debt* (Penguin)

Ghazali, A and Omar, S eds. (1989) *Readings in the Concept and Methodology of Islamic Economics* (Pelanduk Publications)

Giddens, A (1971) *Capitalism and modern social theory—An analysis of the writings of Marx, Durkheim and Max Weber* (Cambridge University Press)

Gifford, P (1991) Christian Fundamentalism and Development, *Review of African Political Economy* 52

Gumbel, N (1994) *Searching Issues* (Kingsway Publications)

Hall, P (1983) *Growth and Development: An Economic Analysis* (Martin Robertson)

Hastings, A (1995) *The Shaping of Prophecy: Passion, Perception and Practicality* (Geoffrey Chapman)

Hebblethwaite, B (1987) *The Incarnation* (Cambridge University Press)

Heiss, MA (1996) *Empire and Nationhood: The United States, Great Britain and Iranian Oil, 1950-1954* (Columbia University Press)

Hewitt, T ed. (1992) *Industrialisation and Development* (Oxford University Press)

Hick, J ed. (1977) *The Myth of God Incarnate* (SCM)

Hubner, H (1984) *Law in Paul's Thought* (T&T Clark)

Hume, B (14 May 1998) *Forgive the poorest their debts—now* (The Times)

Huntington, SP (1996) *The Clash of Civilisations and the Remaking of the World Order* (Touchstone)

Hussain, SS and Ashraf, SA (1979) *Crisis in Muslim Education* (Hodder and Stoughton)

Ibn Kathir (1991) *The Signs Before the Day of Judgement* translated by Khattab, H (Dar Al Taqwa)

Ipgrave, M ed. (2002) *The Road Ahead: A Christian-Muslim Dialogue* (Church House Publishing)

Kahf, M (1994) Budget Deficits and Public Borrowing Instruments in an Islamic Economic System. *The American Journal of Islamic Social Sciences* 11/2

Kee, H (1990) *What Can We Know About Jesus?* (Cambridge University Press)

Khalid, KM (___) *Men Around The Messenger* (Al Manara)

Khan, MA (1997) The Role of Government in the Economy. *The American Journal of Islamic Social Sciences* 14/2

Khan, MAM (1996) The Philosophical Foundations of Islamic Political Economy. *The American Journal of Islamic Social Sciences* 13/3

Khan, WM (1985) *Towards an Interest-free Islamic Economic System: A Theoretical Analysis of Prohibiting Debt Financing* (The Islamic Foundation)

Kooiman, D (1988) *Change of religion as a way to survival. Some source material from 19th-century Travancore, India* in Ufford, PQ and Schoffeleers, M eds. (1988) *Religion and Development: Towards and Integrated Approach* (Free University Press)

Küng, H ed. (1986) *Christianity and the World Religions —Paths of Dialogue with Islam, Hinduism and Buddhism* (Doubleday Publishing)

Kuran, T (1992) 'The Economic System in Contemporary Islamic Thought' in Jomo, KS ed. *Islamic Economic Alternatives. Critical Perspectives and New Directions* (Macmillan)

Langoni, CG (1987) *The Development Crisis: Blueprint for Change* (International Centre for Economic Growth)

Lenin, V (1978) *On Religion* (Progress Publishers)

Lewis, B (1993) *Islam in History* (Open Court Publishing)

Linz, WMA (1996) 'A religious country reflected in its publishing industry' in *LOGOS* (Whurr Publishers) 7/1

Lodhi, MAK ed. (1989) *Islamization of Attitudes and Practices in Science and Technology* (IIIT)

Lohse, B (1966) *A Short History of Christian Doctrine* (Fortress Press)

Lydall, H (1979) *A Theory of Income Distribution* (Clarendon Press)

M Percy, M and Jones, I eds. (2002) *Fundamentalism, Church and Society* (SPCK)

Mack, BL (1993) *The Lost Gospel: The Book of Q & Christian Origins* (Rosemary Pugh Books)

Makdisi, G (1981) *The Rise of Colleges: Institutions of Learning in Islam and the West* (Edinburgh University Press)

Manshipouri, M (1997) Review Article: Islamism, Civil Society and the Democracy Conundrum. *The Muslim World* 87/1

Matar, N (1998) *Islam in Britain: 1558-1685* (Cambridge University Press)

Maw, J (1985) *Twende! A Practical Swahili Course* (Oxford University Press)

Mehmet, O (1990) *Islamic Identity and Development: Studies of the Islamic Periphery* (Routledge)

Melamid, A (1991) *Oil and the Economic Geography of the Middle East and North Africa* (The Darwin Press)

Messer, R (1993) *Does God's Existence Need Proof?* (Oxford University Press)

Metzger, B (1992) *The Text of the New Testament: Its Transmission, Corruption, and Restoration* (Oxford University Press)

Metzger, B (1997) *The Canon Of The New Testament: Its Origin, Significance & Development* (Clarendon Press)

Metzger, B and Coogan, M (1993) *The Oxford Companion to the Bible* (Oxford University Press)

Moberly, W (1998) *Can Balaam's Ass Speak Today? A Case Study in Reading the Old Testament as Scripture* (Grove Books)

Muldoon, J (1979) *Popes, Lawyers and Infidels: The Church and the Non-Christian World 1250-1550* (Liverpool University Press)

Nadawi, SA (1993) *Muhammad The Last Prophet: A model for all time* (UKIA)

Newbigin, L (1989) *The Gospel in Pluralist Society* (SPCK)

Omran, AR (1992) *Family Planning in the Legacy of Islam* (Routledge)

Peerzade, SA (1997) The Definition and Measurement of Poverty: An Integrated Islamic Approach. *The Pakistan Development Review* 36/1

Pramanik, AH (1996) *Muslim world agriculture in Disarray, an Agenda for social development* (International Islamic University)

Qaradawi, Y (1993) *Islamic Awakening between Rejection and Extremism* (IIIT)

Ramsey, M (1980) *Jesus and the Living Past* (Oxford University Press)

Rand, S (1999) A New Start. *Teartimes* 1

Rodinson, M (1974) *Islam and Capitalism* (Penguin)

Rosenthal, F (1970) *Knowledge Triumphant: The Concept of Knowledge in Medieval Islam* (E.J. Brill)

Ruthstöm-Ruin, C (1993) *Beyond Europe: The Globalization of Refugee Aid* (Lund University Press)

Sa'd, M (1995) *The Women of Madina* (Ta-Ha)

Sadeq, AM (1990) *Economic Development in Islam* (Pelanduk Publications)

Schacht, J (1950) *The Origins of Muhammadan Jurisprudence* (Clarendon Press)

Schacht, J (1964) *An Introduction to Islamic Law* (Clarendon Press)

Schoeps, HJ (1988) *Theologie und Geschichte des Judenchristentums* (Hildesheim)

Sells, M (1996) *The Bridge Betrayed: Religion and genocide in Bosnia* (University of California Press)

Sen, A (1997) *On Economic Inequality* (Clarendon Press)

Shackelton, R (1975) *Censure and Censorship: Impediments to Free Publication in the Age of Enlightenment* (The University of Texas at Austin)

Siddiqi, MN (1989) *Tawhid: The Concept and the Process* in Ghazali, A & Omar, S eds. (1989) *Readings in the Concept and Methodology of Islamic Economics* (Pelanduk Publications)

Stevenson, J (1957) *A New Eusebius* (SPCK)

Stewart, F (1989) Basic Needs Strategies, Human Rights, and the Right to Development. *Human Rights Quarterly* 11

Sultan, A (1997) WTO Successor to GATT: Implications for the Muslim World. *The American Journal of Islamic Social Sciences* 14/2

Swinburne, R (1996) *Is There a God?* (Oxford University Press)

Syrquin, M (1998) *Modern Economic (Endogenous) Growth and Development* in Coricelli, F *et al.* eds. (1998) *New Theories in Growth and Development* (Macmillan)

Thatcher, A (1990) *Truly a Person, Truly God* (SPCK)

Tibawi, AL (1979) *Islamic Education: Its Traditions and Modernization into the Arab National Systems* (Luzac and Company)

Todaro, MP (1997) *Economic Development* (Longman)

Ufford, PQ and Schoffeleers, M eds. (1988) *Religion and Development: Towards and Integrated Approach* (Free University Press)

Ul-Haq, I (1996) *Economic Doctrines of Islam: A Study in the Doctrines of Islam and their Implications for Poverty, Employment, and Economic Growth* (IIIT)

UNHCR (1993) *The State of the World's Refugees—The Challenge of Protection* (Penguin)

Unwin, T ed. (1994) *Atlas of World Development* (John Wiley and Sons)

US Department of State (11 March 2008) *Country Reports on Human Rights Practices–2007* (Bureau of Democracy, Human Rights, and Labor)

Vatikiotis, PJ (1987) *Islam and the State* (Routledge)

Vermes, G (1973) *Jesus the Jew* (SCM)

Vermes, G (1995) *The Dead Seas Scrolls in English* (Penguin)

Watt, M (1968) *What is Islam?* (Longman, Green and Company)

Watt, M (1991) *Muslim-Christian Encounters* (Routledge)

Wax, E (23 September 2002) *Islam Attracting Many Survivors of Rwanda Genocide—Jihad Is Taught as 'Struggle to Heal'* (Washington Foreign Post Service)

Weber, M (1974) *The Protestant Ethic and the Spirit of Capitalism* (Unwin University Books)

Wenham, D (1995) *Paul—Follower of Jesus or Founder of Christianity* (Eerdmans)

Whiston, W (1992) *The Works of Josephus: Complete and Unabridged in One Volume* (Peabody)

Wilson, R (1995) *Economic Development in the Middle East* (Routledge)

Yusuf, H (19 June 2002) *Islam has a progressive tradition too* (The Guardian)

Printed in the United Kingdom by
Lightning Source UK Ltd., Milton Keynes
137285UK00001B/78/P